T0193900

AuthorHouse™ UK
1663 Liberty Drive
Bloomington, IN 47403 USA
www.authorhouse.co.uk
Phone: 0800.197.4150

Published by AuthorHouse 02/05/2016

ISBN: 978-1-5049-4092-4 (sc)
ISBN: 978-1-5049-4093-1 (hc)
ISBN: 978-1-5049-4094-8 (e)

Luciano Manara

The Son of a She Wolf

authorHOUSE®

Ye were not form'd to live the life of brutes

but virtue to pursue and knowledge high

(*Dante, Inferno XXVI*)

Dedication

To my ancestors whose teaching, mostly silent,

and care led me through hardship to reward.

Acknowledgements

Judy Baggott's invaluable laundering of quite a few "mud spots" in this rustic author's self taught English is greatly appreciated.

I'm grateful to the Municipality of The City of Belluno for permission (*Concessione n.2/2015*) to reproduce from its Historical Archives the views of the Aristide Gabelli public school (*Fototeca, Album 34-02-41*) and the ONB building in Segato Street (*Fondo V.A. Doglioni b. 42*). My special thanks to Ms. Orietta Ceiner, Head of the Archives, for her patient assistance.

Many of the main facts and figures of WWII in this book have been freely borrowed from the digital Encyclopaedia Britannica (*Encyclopaedia Britannica Deluxe Edition, Chicago 2010*).

About the author

Luciano Manara, Italian, born in 1935, earned his
M.D. degree *summa cum laude* at Milan University,
did his military service in the Italian Medical Corps,
and went on to a lifelong international research
career, first as a "bench scientist", later with
managerial responsibilities. His endeavors earned
him several domestic and foreign awards. He also
did some teaching and wrote scientific papers and
books, and articles for the lay press (scientific
dissemination).
Since his retirement to his native countryside in
2005, he has dedicated himself to gardening,
cultivating fruit trees and vegetables.

Afterthoughts

An old man approaching the end of his long

journey retires to the Italian countryside where he

spent most of his first ten years, before and

throughout World War II: He sets out to

rediscover his boyhood there. He also rethinks

major events of those times, as perceived with his

later learning. That offers him further insight on

how his life evolved elsewhere as well on why his

motherland's enviable wealth of creativity and

natural and historical beauty is still marred by

persistently fractured politics.

Contents

1. Reviving Myths and…War!

   Scholars of ancient Greek literature praise Plutarch especially for his *"Parallel Lives"*, an account of similar Greek and Roman nobles. One of these paired biographies is about Theseus, the mythical hero who killed the Minotaur and founded Athens, and Romulus, founder and first king of Rome. Livy, a most respected historian in ancient Rome, reports the legend about how Romulus escaped drowning with his male twin at birth Remo, as ordered by their grandfather's brother Amulius; they were rescued by a herdsman and then breast-fed by his wife whose nickname was "she-wolf" because of her part-time job as a sex worker. Yet official, generally accepted - and taught in schools - Roman folklore, insists even up to current times that an actual she-wolf arrived on the scene first to help and nurse the twins, who only later were looked after by the herdsman and his wife, who in this version becomes a pious woman.
When in the late 1920s Mussolini's Fascist Italy dictated Italian youth's patriotic education, boys and girls, ranked by age, were assigned names and wore uniforms. At Saturday morning outdoor meetings and on certain important occasions, like the anniversary of Rome's foundation, the boys in the first rank - the lowest, for those aged up to eight - were known as "Sons of the She-wolf" *(Figli della Lupa);* of course they were told the politically correct version of the Romulus myth, rather than Livy's account!

   Luciano, an Italian boy born in September 1935, filed away a few unusually early-in-life memories, but none about when he first donned his uniform. Photographs, however, (one on the cover of this book) show him as early as two, dressed up in the regulation black shirt, white belt with two wide straps crossing on the chest and passing over each shoulder, and black fez. The fez was adorned with the ancient Roman symbol of the Capitoline Wolf suckling twin infants and the

1

huge chest buckle was shaped like the letter "M", somewhat resembling that in Mussolini's signature.

The older boys (8 to 14 years) were called *"Balilla"*. A teenager hero of this nickname (actual name Gianbattista Perasso) started the 1746 Genoa popular uprising against the occupying Austrians, by tossing a rock toward an officer; the invaders were forced out of town. That was a forerunner of the 19th-century *Risorgimento* (rising again), the process largely interpreted as some sort of myth by Fascism, that freed the Italian states from foreign domination and united them politically in one sole nation in 1861, as a kingdom under the Savoia dynasty whose reign, in northwest Italy, formerly consisted mostly of Piedmont. *Balilla* was also the title of a Fascist youth-devoted patriotism-inspiring weekly magazine for the young folk; Luciano preserved some World War II issues, the front pages completely covered with comic strips. There were funny color drawings by leading domestic cartoonists of the day, irreverently depicting a dummy George VI, regularly scared to death (e.g. by German bombers); the British king would seek protection by his Prime Minister Winston Churchill (portrayed puffing at his Havana and looking ugly). Later on, in primary school, Luciano, like any other boy whose father had left to war, proudly wore a pin saying: "God curse the English!". A lifelong friend of Luciano was Horace E. Dobbs and Horace, in Britain, was taught at school that he should hate the Italians. In the long run, to the two former boys' and everybody else's good luck and satisfaction, it didn't end up that way. In the second half of the 20th century Europe, despite occasional quarrels, was basically peaceful; its borders had become purely virtual for its dwellers, enjoying the convenience of a single currency for business and leisure. Now grown up, Luciano saw much of Horace, a renowned writer, underwater photographer and conservationist and they shared many unforgettable visits to sea-beds around the world.

Luciano was five when Italy entered World War II and his perceptions of the events of those times of conflict obviously heavily influenced his developing personality. Because of his father's job - Mario Manara was then a dedicated young Fascist executive charged with managing provincial sections of the national foundation for youth welfare and patriotic education ONB (*Opera Nazionale Balilla*) - the boy lived for some time in different places scattered throughout his home country. That summer he was in Pietra Marazzi (known familiarly just as Pietra meaning "stone"), his ancestors' village in northwest Italy, with its fewer than 400 souls. The first hills of lower Piedmont can be seen rising, just left of the River Tanaro bordering the Marengo plain, the site of the Austrians' defeat by Napoleon on 14 June 1800, where over 13,000 soldiers died out of about 60,000 who fought. One hundred and forty years after that carnage, Luciano witnessed Mussolini's announcement that Italy was taking active part into what was to turn into the largest and bloodiest conflict of history, costing about fifty million lives, to a large extent civilians.

On 10 June 1940, around 5 pm, Pietra Marazzi's antique municipal building's courtyard, fitted with national flags and loudspeakers, was crowded as never before and so was the adjacent square facing the church. The silent attendees didn't have to wait too long for the Duce's thundering, unmistakable voice to shout out short sharp phrases, with short pauses in between. And the fatal word came: war! Luciano, like everybody else was stunned - as usual - by the very sound of Mussolini's speech, no matter what it was about. Most interpretations of that happening, of course, were far removed from what Luciano and the other attending toddlers understood, and they soon resumed their noisy playing around; but he noticed something unusual. At the formal "Fascist Saturday" meetings Luciano had attended elsewhere in different towns, while donning his Son of the She-wolf uniform, the adults too wore uniforms, including a black shirt; one of them would generally deliver a speech, followed by a standing ovation. But that day in Pietra, no black shirts, no uniforms were seen: a speechless, petrified crowd listened in silence to the loudspeakers echoing the hurrahs of the endless multitude around *Palazzo Venezia* in Rome, from whose balcony the nation's leader was addressing the Italians. Many of those at the meeting in Pietra still remembered well the tragedy of two and a half decades before, World War I; quite a few who could have been at the meeting did not make it back home from that war, which saw 600,000 Italians dead.

Shortly after that Mussolini's epochal speech, possibly the following day, Luciano (an often exuberant boy at the time, always looking for new ways to have fun with his pals and to impress them) had an idea. He gathered a little crowd of his peers in front of his mother's father's (grandpa Giuseppe) house, which faced the village main street, and briefed them. Then Luciano went upstairs, came out on a balcony whose flag-stand in the balustrade he fitted with a broom he had taken along and began to address his public right away. The speaker and his audience soon started to have great fun, even more so since the "public", unlike the local attendees of Mussolini's broadcasted speech, applauded almost at Luciano's every other word, just like the great multitude in Rome. This understandably excited Luciano, whose grip on his supporters soon grew, and more kids at play nearby were drawn by the increasingly noisy happening to join in. Eventually the unusually vociferous and numerous gathering of local children drew the attention of adults. Several closed blinds (to provide shade from the darts of sunlight of a late summer afternoon) of houses in the neighbourhood facing south-west were opened by the occupants, inquiring what was going on; some other adults who happened to go by stopped, amused; customers waiting at the barber's shop came over too and had a look. No doubt, most of the adults realized what had inspired this unprecedented kind of play; some may also have reasoned it wasn't politically correct, in spite of its unquestionable innocence. Nobody, though, bothered to stop the children; nobody, that is, until …. Joe came!

At the turn of the 20th century, Giuseppe Cattaneo (better known as Joe, when he returned home after making true his good share of the American dream), just over 20, left Italy and a hopeless prospect of misery as an illiterate subsistence farmer. He shortly joined some compatriots in Tennessee, but then started cotton and vegetable farming on his own, and soon managed to have his wife Teresa and first child Gemma (the elder sister of Luciano's mother Leonora, known as Nora) join him. Though lacking any education, Joe was fairly at ease with numbers and gifted with intuitiveness. He and Teresa had been used to hard work in the fields since school age and just carried on that way in the new world, but there they relied profitably on Afro-American labor to run their farm. The Cattaneos, like the other immigrant farmers from Northern Italy in the area (Frayser, North of Memphis), lived in peace within the predominantly Italian community which was also home to many blacks. Joe and Teresa spared their offspring, who attended school, from having to join in the hard work. Gemma shuttled the black helpers to the farm and back home; she drove a light truck, possibly some version of the Ford Model T, the "mythical" car that helped America into the automobile age. It became a part of popular culture and the subject of songs and jokes. John, the second (American-) born, went to nearby Memphis to help his uncle, Teresa's brother, who had a grocery store. Nora, the third child also born there in 1912, was grown up enough six

4

years later to prove a blessing, giving support to the whole family suffering from the dreadful epidemic of influenza, to which she proved immune (the so-called Spanish flu infected 500 million people in 1918-19 and claimed the lives of one in five of those who caught it). Eleven-year-old American-born Nora was brought to Italy by the repatriating family; however, she had innumerable, mostly enjoyable memories of her birth-place and its customs, like the jazz bands on the Mississippi riverboats, the blacks being baptized in the Wolf River, the search for eggs on Easter Monday, the prison inmates working in chain-gangs along the railroad. Luciano, as a child, was enchanted by his mother's vivid recollections and often asked her to tell him more; he too started soon to dream of America! When Joe returned to Italy In 1922, he settled in Pietra Marazzi where he bought a vast house (formerly belonging to a once-prosperous eminent local family, the Brezzi), including a majestic cellar which he fitted with huge oak wine casks; he also purchased some fertile land in the plain and an extensive area on the hill overlooking the village, where he had several terraces carved out and planted a vineyard later known as *il giardino* (the garden) for his almost obsessive care to keep it cleverly cultivated and weed-free. Joe also owned a three-storey apartment building in nearby Alessandria, the main town of one of the six provinces of Piedmont and home of the world famous Borsalino factory at the time; name anyone, from U. S. President Roosevelt to the gangster's king Al Capone: all wore its hats.

Giuseppe Borsalino had set up in Alessandria the first artisan workshop for the production of felt hats in the second half of the 19th century; his son Teresio boosted the family business to a remarkable industrial scale. That was a blessing for the local economy: hundred of jobs were created. Magnanimous Teresio, whose life-sized portrait hangs in the lecture hall of the local hospital he substantially contributed to, built the city a new aqueduct and a special clinic for treating respiratory diseases (suffered by many of his workers, because of inhaling rabbit fur, the raw material for producing felt). The Borsalino Company was successful until the 1940s, when the hat business declined and none of the dynasty's heirs managed to start it anew after the war. The trademark was sold and has since been applied to a wide variety of luxury items in addition to hats - ties, clothing, watches and perfumes. Nothing of the impressive old factory is left in town except, in its former head offices, a museum dedicated to the history of the hat. Luciano also learned the Borsalino story from his mother; as a teenager she was sent to learn embroidery from

Alessandria's French nuns and often admired the *Borsalines*, the young women hired at the factory, mostly locally, going to and coming out of work; they were renowned for their charm and fashionable apparel - a few of those chicks married wealthy entrepreneurs or professionals!

From the balcony, where he had mounted to harangue his companions, Luciano could see the flat stretch of Via Roma (the village main street), for about three hundred yards, till where it turned left downhill; there he spotted the two oxen first, then the cart they pulled, which was enough to know grandfather Joe was on his way home and would show up too in a moment. In that hilly area oxen (not usually horses) were the sole power source for farming; only in June, after the wheat was harvested (by scything), a threshing machine and its power supply, a steam engine, both horse-drawn, were brought to the village for a few days. Luciano that year had enjoyed watching the threshing operations and seeing the hay being pressed into bales which, stored under a huge porch next to grandfather Joe's stable, for a while became one of his (and his friends') favorite playgrounds. Formerly, while living in town, the boy had been shown a newspaper image of Mussolini, bare chested, on a threshing machine: a celebration of the *battaglia del grano* (the battle for wheat), intended to foster domestic farming in Italy which was enduring sanctions by the League of Nations after invading Ethiopia in 1936.
Either pulling a cart or ploughing, oxen used to be driven in a way that fascinated Luciano. In the first place they were given their own names, different from those usually adopted for other domestic animals or pets; the bovines' caretaker at work was supposed to address them continuously, repeating their name and, like a sort of arousing, encouragement or scolding, the contrasting commands (in the local dialect): "Come here; go there!". One could easily guess the mood of the oxen's driver by the way he addressed his animals. That day wasn't one of Joe's best, since his angry shouting to Barthò and Cavallee could be heard from a distance. The juniors listening to Luciano's speech were also forewarned as, at the sight of Joe Luciano had been struck dumb. The crowd quickly disassembled before Joe came close enough to figure anything out, but he didn't bother to ask. He would hardly have noticed the boy and his broom on the distant balcony, since Luciano, as soon as he spotted him, quickly went downstairs. Nobody took the risk of upsetting Joe by telling him

6

about his grandchild's performance. Thus we can assume that Luciano walked off uncensored that time!

Luciano remembers well another event later the same year in the courtyard of the village municipal building, but this time it did not suggest any game he could play later with his friends. He had followed his grandmother Giuseppina (his father's mother), who was carrying several copper pans there. All sorts of metal ware was piling up in front of the building as the village residents brought it in; Joe gave up the masterly crafted iron fence of his courtyard. These government-solicited donations in the public interest were meant to contribute to national economic self-sufficiency and independence for Italy in the face of sanctions. A few years earlier Luciano's mother, in a similar setting, had traded her own and her husband's gold wedding rings for two iron ones: that was the *Oro alla Patria* (Gold for the Nation) campaign.

The war had caught Luciano's father in Pietra on temporary leave he had asked for while waiting for a new assignment. He intended to complete his exams in Turin University and get the degree in economics. He was encouraged to do so since, by tradition, combatant students enjoyed special indulgence when tested. That was known as the "war 18", 18 points out of 30 being the minimum score to pass an exam, which Mario did by always donning his uniform as second lieutenant in the *Bersaglieri* (marksmen) corps. Sincere as he had been raised, Mario never concealed to anybody, including his family, how he managed to complete his studies so swiftly. Luciano hardly figured out what his father had done and was even more puzzled by somebody addressing him as "Doctor"; it was hard for the five-year-old boy - who eventually became a real medical doctor himself - that Italian law allows anybody who gets a university degree to use the title of doctor, though of course by no means the right to deal with patients.

2. Urban Dweller

Mostly because of the war, Luciano spent a good deal of his childhood in roughish rural settings: unpaved roads led to Pietra Marazzi, his ancestors' village crossed by streets that were no better, where houses, including the otherwise comfortable homes of the wealthiest and best educated families, lacked tap water and indoor lavatories! The harsh but genuine style of living in the growing, tangible poverty brought about by the second world conflict no doubt widened the boy's perceptions of what really mattered for survival in those difficult times: an incomparable formative experience. However, prior to that, while life in his home country was still enjoyable, he had been raised in urban, developed areas. He had taken his first steps in Asti, where he was born, the main town of one of the six provinces of Piedmont, renowned for its sweet, white, sparkling wine "*Asti Spumante*". True worldwide connoisseurs, however, praise the Italian red wines *Barolo* and *Barbaresco* - both from Piedmont too - with their rivals, Tuscany's *Chianti* and *Montalcino*.

Luciano learned later on, at the *liceo* (high school whose curriculum gives priority to the humanities), about Asti's most eminent citizen, Vittorio Alfieri, a tragic poet of the second half of the 18th century whose main theme was the overthrow of tyranny (he also wrote a poem celebrating American independence). Alfieri's dramas nurtured the national spirit of Italy which, one hundred years later, pervaded the noble patriots who fought to free the Italian states from foreign domination and unite them politically in a single nation. That was the *Risorgimento*, acknowledged by historians as an aristocratic and bourgeois revolution that failed to fully involve the masses but, in the Fascist era, Luciano was taught about it at school as a myth of popular uprising, to foster sentiments of national unity and identity. The development in Italy of a similar common sentiment of devotion to the home country was definitely compromised when the second world conflict turned into a further-dividing, most disgraceful sort of civil war. As if that were not enough, shortly after the war was over in Italy, a referendum in 1946 - whose legality some disputed - decided in favor of a republic, with a slight majority, most of the voters from the northern parts of the country. Persistent divisions and penury of shared civil values still seem to prevent Italians enjoying even a tenuous sense of nationhood, which has been lengthily and wrongly perceived simply as yet another Fascist heritage. These major shortcomings are reflected in the country's persisting World War I times-like fractured politics, delaying the structural reforms which hopefully one day should bring Italy closer to the more developed western democracies. Meanwhile, scores of jovial Italians in the third millennium do feel strongly committed to the same nation and its undisputed sporting record, each time their national soccer team enters the World Cup contest!

Having moved away from Asti when he was only three, arguably Luciano was spared any significant imprinted memory of those years, even if at times he felt he did recall minor events and objects that his parents or relatives might also have mentioned. Presumably, for instance, having been told when he was four or five about himself and his environment earlier in life, the boy later on was liable to confuse these items reported to him with his own original impressions: a sort of "false" memory. Decades later, in his professional life, Luciano learnt about research on these false memories which seem to be more common during early childhood. While in his case only innocent fakes of no concern were involved, there has been growing preoccupation about the malicious induction of false memories, especially for their bearing in certain types of trials.

Thus the two foremost, lifelong decisive events which occurred in his birth place he was told later on: one of course being born there, the other surviving pneumonia he caught when not yet two. In 1935 infant mortality was still over 15%, as compared to 0,4 in the years Two thousands.

After many years Luciano happened to visit Asti and was shown, from the opposite side of the street, a little nice villa surmounted by a small tower. Not only did he recognize his former home, but he described a terrace at the back of the building which he could not have seen from where he was standing. It may well be that he had seen it before all in a photo which, however, he never did find. That house had been bought with his mother's dowry, at Luciano's birth, and was sold shortly afterwards (in 1938), when the family relocated in Ancona where Luciano's father was given a new assignment. The proceeds of that sale went into saving bonds of the Kingdom of Italy which by the end of the war were worth nothing!

Ancona, the capital of the Marche region in central Italy, with its harbor on the Adriatic Sea, sits on the farthest branch of land that comes down from the Conero massif, part of the Apennine mountain range which forms the physical backbone of peninsular Italy. The place offers one more of the countless enjoyable examples in the country of a variety of landforms within a limited area. Immediately north of Ancona the eastward-looking seaside consists of typical Adriatic flat sandy beaches, bathed by long stretches of shallow water out into the sea, whereas the southern city limits continue into a rocky coast steeply descending deeper into the sea from Mount Conero; westward are gently rising green hills stretching out to the horizon. Luciano understandably was hardly impressed by the noteworthy ancient landmarks in the town, like the marble arch of the Roman emperor Trajan, but unquestionably he remembered quite a few places he enjoyed, such as the bather-friendly shore in Palombina, a township less than a couple of miles from downtown Ancona, where Luciano's family settled first, just across the main Adriatic highway facing the sea. At the airport in Falconara, a little further north of Palombina, the boy had close views of airplanes he had never seen before. There was also the grand hotel *Passetto* (actually its reputed restaurant) on the hill overlooking Ancona, an occasional family destination on Sundays. At that restaurant Luciano, who had been repeatedly seriously ill and off his food in Asti, took a fancy to a local dish of lasagne, the *Vincisgrassi*. To the relief of his formerly aggrieved parents, the sea climate seemed favorable to their growing son; they may have toasted with *Verdicchio* (though both of them started to drink, moderately at meals, only much later in life), a white table wine typical of the region, also well known and welcome elsewhere.

Luciano boarded at least two ships moored in Ancona's port. The *San Giorgio,* a former obsolete armored cruiser of the 1911 Italo-Turkish war and World War I, had been reconstructed in 1937 and transformed into a large monitor craft for the defence of the Mediterranean African ports of the Italian colony of Libya. On 28 June 1940, the anti-aircraft guns of the ship, moored in Tobruk, mistakenly

11

shot down the plane carrying Italo Balbo, one of Mussolini's four closest co-leaders (the *Quadrumviri*) in the "Fascist Revolution" of 1922 and world-acclaimed pioneer of commercial transatlantic flights. It was its cargo of bananas from the Italian colonies more than the other ship itself that impressed Luciano; with war looming, those exotic fruits were about to disappear from the Italian markets, where they were still absent for quite a while after World War II.

In Ancona Luciano was taken to the movies for the first time and saw Walt Disney's prime feature-length cartoon "*Snow White and the Seven Dwarfs*", widely acclaimed by critics and audiences. It was released in 1937 and was the first full-length traditionally-animated feature film produced in history. Traditional animation, the dominant production method prior to today's computer techniques, involved drawing each frame by hand! Unfortunately, the boy, who was only about four at the time, was frightened by some of the Wicked Queen's scenes, and the show turned into a disturbing experience; he didn't complain or seek reassuring help at the time - he wasn't in his parents' company - but nightmares followed for a while and Mom and Dad couldn't figure out right away why. In view of that problem, though, they were surprised some time later when Luciano was not scared or upset as an eye witness of a spectacular accident involving several cars on the Adriatic highway. It was at late sunset, just in front of the house in Palombina that his family was sharing with its owners. Neither the drivers nor the passengers, including some nuns (one hardly stopped a moment to send God prayers of thanks!), suffered any injury; they all gathered inside, welcomed by the residents in sympathy. The place turned unusually lively. The badly damaged cars were towed to a corner of the ample garden and sat there for some time, to Luciano's delight. Over the next few days, he often ran down to that corner and had many long, close encounters with those much loved wrecked vehicles; he was lucky that he did not hurt himself with broken glass or any other potentially harmful item a boy would hardly resist touching!

When Luciano's family moved from Palombina they took an apartment in a building in downtown Ancona, and that became his playground. In his parent's ample bedroom there was a large vertical mirror. One day the boy was playing in front of it: he loved practicing military commands like he had seen a Fascist youth unit do (they were equipped with small muskets, miniature replicas, but otherwise identical to the World War I Carcano 91 Model; his father had got him one). Twenty-four years later, Luciano happened to live in the USA and tragically recalled the firearm he had been playing with in Ancona: in a warehouse in Dallas, Texas, next to where President J.F. Kennedy had been shot dead on 22 November 1963, the police had found an old Italian-made shoulder firearm and named it.

From a window in the room with the mirror, Luciano could look at a balcony of a building fairly close, where he had spotted a girl, presumably of his age, playing. That day he managed to attract the girl's attention, by peacockishly showing off his musket! It was a curious (Freudian?) way of trying to make friends! In any case the boy did not remember meeting the girl, or anyone of his age, during his short stay in Ancona (hardly two years between 1938-40), neither had he attended kindergarten. Yet he remembered several adult friends of his family he first met there. One of them, Davide, he saw again and again, elsewhere during the war and later on throughout his adult life. He developed a lasting special relationship with him which, however, remained emotionally deeply rooted in each other's feelings of a four- to eight-year-old boy with a grown-up man.

Rosetta and Davide Lajolo, both from Piedmont and recently married, but with no children as yet, lived next door to Luciano's parents in the same apartment building in downtown Ancona. Davide, then 26, a former student of the *Plana* high school in the town of Alessandria, Piedmont (the same school Luciano attended many years later) was a journalist in charge of press relations for the local Fascist Federation, a job he had got from Luciano's Dad Mario, after returning from the Spanish Civil War (1936–39). There he fought, with other Italian volunteer militiamen, contributing to Francisco Franco's Nationalists' eventual victory against the Soviet-backed republicans. When Davide interviewed adult Luciano (in the Italian Communist Party weekly "*Giorni Vie Nuove* of 8 May 1974) he recalls him briefly as a toddler in Ancona: "*.....He too comes from Monferrato* [the hills of South-East Piedmont] *and is familiar with its people and places, though now he looks at them with a scientist's eye... That sight* [Luciano's] *was enough for both of us to feel we were back home there. Luciano still frowns like, when a child, holding a folder between his chest and arm, he would tell me he wanted to study to be a leader, then say good-bye and walk out aloof, without waiting for any reply...*". Luciano's childish perception of Davide was of a model warrior leading his men to victory: besides admiring him in his uniform, the boy's preferred game, when in Davide's apartment, was to be allowed to take out his medals and handgun ammunitions from a drawer. Following Mussolini's dismissal by the Grand Council of Fascism on 25 July 1943 and the subsequent events resulting in the Germans taking over northern and most of central Italy on September 8, Davide joined the Communist partisans of the anti-Fascist Resistance in the hills of Piedmont, and was nicknamed *Ulisse*, likewise the Latin name for Ulysses, Homer's hero in his epic poem "The Odyssey". After the war, Davide was appointed editor of *Unità*, the official newspaper of the Italian Communist Party whose Central Committee he later entered, while also serving three times as Member of Parliament. These duties, implying constant political writing, did not prevented him fostering and displaying his creativity in novels and poems (whose principal themes were the partisan war and his native hills of Piedmont with their uses and legends). He is known abroad for "*An absurd vice*", a critical biography of Cesare Pavese, his friend and fellow writer, also from Piedmont.   .

Luciano's further recollection of meeting adults in Ancona was a kind of fairy tale come true. A beautiful lady, who had no children at the time, came for a few days to pay a visit to his parents. She took him on a long walk downtown and bought all the toys the boy would ask for! Not only did they return home literally loaded, but a few bulky items were delivered later on. Was that a dream transformed into a false memory as sometime happens? By no means: as an adult Luciano met Marquise Elena Saporiti and her sons again and again; in recalling the episode with the lady, he tended to blush! That incident adds up to Luciano's memory of the comfortable, decorous, rewarding urban experience in Ancona, although it was only short. The boy enjoyed the living conditions in the country which, in the previous few years of the Fascist era, had just reached their best. Regrettably a change for the worse was on its way, in view of Mussolini's increasingly close ties with Adolf Hitler's Germany (resented and feared, even by many Fascists). The Duce was already badly entangled, enough not to avoid soon involving Italy in a disastrous war. A shameful, tangible premonition came with the Hitler-inspired anti-Semitic laws in Italy in 1938. Jews were condemned as unpatriotic, excluded from government jobs, and forbidden to marry "Aryans".
Some of Luciano's blurred impressions surfaced from the depths of his memory quite a few years later, when he learned what they meant: why had his aunt Tina, a voluntary Red Cross nurse, complained that

Doctor Finzi (a typically Jewish Italian name like Levi) had left Alessandria's hospital? Why was his Dad struggling to obtain baptism certificates of all the ancestors he knew of ?

In Germany in November that year things turned very bad right away for Jews, with "The Night of Broken Glass". Nazis attacked Jewish persons and property, synagogues were burned, rioters ransacked and looted Jewish businesses and vandalized Jewish hospitals, homes, schools, and cemeteries. After this their survival there became impossible. In Italy, however, Fascist persecution of Jews under the racial laws, as reported by the historian Renzo De Felice, a former Communist, was fortunately fairly "bland, the Italian way"; nothing like the infamous German night could have happened, as he wrote, "in a society historically immune from the anti-Semitic virus". For a while, the Italian Jews did not seem to be under any special threat, but after 8 September 1943, when the Germans had taken over the northern and most of the central part of the country, they were faced with ruin.

The Italian writer and chemist Primo Levi (1919-1987) - he too from Piedmont - renowned for his autobiographical account of and reflections on survival in the Nazi concentration camps (" *If This Is a Man*"; 1947), graduated in Turin in 1941. As he recounts in "*The Periodic Table*" (1975, consisting of 21 assays each named for a chemical element, a metaphor encompassing the physical, chemical, and moral realms), in 1942 the young Levi was working unworriedly as a scientist in a Milan pharmaceutical lab; in the second half of the following year when the German troops took full control, he attempted to join his friends in the hills of Piedmont to connect with the Resistance movement, but was captured and sent to Auschwitz. Only a minority of Italian Jews who had not moved to safety abroad in time escaped deportation by hiding away from their homes, in some place where they could generally trust people's loyalty. Several found secure refuge in Catholic institutions and even in the Vatican State (nonetheless Pope Pius XII was charged with not officially raising his authoritative voice in defence against their persecution). Only a few were lucky enough to avoid any problem by simply living their normal life. That was the case for Ilia Boffi's family; they owned the first bookstore in Alessandria which operated undisturbed throughout wartime. The beautiful Ilia had been Luciano's 3rd-grade school mate in Pietra Marazzi; he had fallen desperately in love with her, but so desperately that he never dared think of letting her know.

3. Paradise Lost?

In 1935, the year of Luciano's birth, Fascist Italy, then better established as a colonial power with the conquest of Ethiopia, had reached its peak - it was destined to sink soon into the abysmal calamity of World War II. From the age of three to five years the child who tasted life in his home country in the late 1930s, as the times were starting to hit hard, couldn't help feeling he had lost a paradise. He knew though, no matter how vaguely, that Italy had already been through troublesome times before. Grandmother Giuseppina had shared with him some of her frightening memories of riots and Communist raids in Tortona, the town in Piedmont near Pietra, where she had given birth to Luciano's father Mario in 1907. That was a period of social and political unrest, with strikes and tumults, following World War I, which had left Italy with large debts, inflation and unemployment - thousands of soldiers were demobilized.

One bit of Giuseppina's moral legacy, typical of her attitudes in those difficult moments no longer subject to the rule of law, was once brought to Luciano's attention by his Dad. She had gone to a shoemaker's shop with her son and daughter: both needed new shoes. The appalled shopkeeper welcomed the newcomers coolly: a sign on the counter displaying hammer and sickle read: "All items must be sold at 80% discount". Giuseppina walked out without buying anything! Italy, which many feared could succumb to Bolshevization - in the wake of the 1917 overthrow of the Russian Tsar's imperial government by the Bolsheviks - was widely plagued by "red" violence which, however, was soon opposed and eventually overcome by the no less brutal Fascist violence.

The "Fascist Revolution" of 1922, which marked the movement's advent to power, caused no bloodshed, however, because of its widespread, growing public acceptance, at least as the only way out of those troubled times. The "March on Rome" (28 October 1922, whose yearly celebrations Luciano attended in his junior Fascist uniform) turned into a victory parade, since King Victor Emmanuel III appointed Benito Mussolini, aged 39, Prime Minister, the youngest in Italian history. Actually Mussolini, unlike the marching, militarized Fascist squads in black shirts and their leaders, travelled to Rome from Milan by train on the morning of October 30, reportedly in a sleeping car!

Mussolini's clever and contemptuous manoeuvring meant that the minority position of the National Fascist Party in the deeply divided Parliament was no problem at all; with a large margin it approved the new electoral law under which, in the subsequent elections in April 1924, the Fascists had 65% of the votes and two thirds of the parliamentary seats. Even so, the assassination of the Socialist representative Giacomo Matteotti, whose moral responsibility Mussolini admitted, nearly compromised the Fascist electoral success and offered his persistent disparate opponents an opportunity to overthrow him; apparently, though, they didn't earn the King's support for their would-be *coup de main*. By 1925 Mussolini had virtually extinguished Parliament by declaring himself *Duce* (from the ancient Roman title *Dux*, meaning leader). Though he is regarded as a dictator by most popular historians, it should not go unnoticed that the Grand Council of Fascism, as well as the King, stayed in place, with the power to fire him - as they did eventually, though too late to spare the country an even worse fate in World War II. Mussolini generally dealt with political dissenters by placing them under arrest and exiling them to small Italian islands.

Up to the fourth grade of elementary school, Luciano learned of several developments to be proud of in contemporary Italy. At home he was told more: they reflected the political stability brought about by Fascism in the second half of the 1920s that pulled Italy gradually out of the post-War I aftermath towards progress. Important domestic public works were undertaken. The taming of the *Pontine* marshes in central Italy in the Lazio region, not far from Rome, which for centuries had been a malaria-infested swampland, was a ten-year project (1928-1939) acclaimed the world over, and created a productive agricultural area and five new towns, thanks to a system of massive pumps and canals. Thirty thousand sharecroppers, mostly from northern Italy, who had lost their livelihood, settled in the reclaimed marshes; the government placed about 2000 families in two-storey colonial houses, known as *poderi*, assigning each an oven, a plough and other agricultural tools, a stable, some cows, and several hectares of land. Other developments included a substantial increase in waterpower-generated electricity, railroads and, in northern Italy, fast motorways. This created much-needed jobs. Land reforms and incentives for agriculture resulted in increased production, especially of cereals: wheat imports were reduced by 75% in 1925. Aviation and automobile industries flourished, pursuing cutting-edge technologies. Italian planes and cars set world speed records and gained top places in international competitions. Since 1930 Mussolini had repeatedly appealed for a popular car, so to help the Italians get one. Senator Giovanni Agnelli, the owner of FIAT, the biggest Italian car maker, announced in June 1936 the 500 Type A best known as the *Topolino* (literally "little mouse", but actually the Italian name for Disney's hero Mickey Mouse; it was the smallest automobile in the world - a little over three meters long, with two seats, and a 569 cubic centimetre four-cylinder engine yielding 13 hp! In spite of its relatively high cost, i.e. 20 times the average monthly wage of a specialized worker, it sold well. The price of the Volkswagen Beatle, which Adolf Hitler, following Mussolini's example, had ordered from Ferdinand Porsche, was only five times a similar worker's pay in Germany. The production of the improved *Topolino* model resumed after the war, up to total of well over 500,000 cars. Luciano's father owned one for a short while, but sold it when the war began, to his son's great disappointment.

Pre-World War II Fascist Italy was marked by further progress otherwise. Youth welfare, physical and patriotic education were promoted: sport, summer camps at the seaside and in the mountains, organized through a specially established institution (*Opera Nazionale Balilla* - ONB), were genuinely popular, but not obligatory. Another institution (*Opera Nazionale Maternità Infanzia* - ONMI) was designed for the protection and care of women before and during childbirth and of their newborn babies and small children; it provided assistance for worker mothers in particular, and those less well off. Mussolini successfully fought the Sicilian Mafia and settled the Vatican question, still pending from the previous century (Lateran Treaty of 1939). The Pope, whose Roman Holy See was recognized as a sovereign state, obtained substantial privileges, including recognition of church weddings as valid in civil law, religious education in national schools, and freedom for lay Catholic organizations. Considerable efforts were made in those years to make Italians of every social class aware of the country's immense wealth of art and culture, from ancient Rome to the modern age.

Thanks to the government-supervised economic policy, Italy largely avoided the Great Depression which hit more industrialized nations, following the catastrophic collapse of the New York stock market in October 1929. Fascist economic nationalism also drastically curtailed the number of emigrants (over 600,000 a year before 1914, ten times less in 1930). These achievements earned Mussolini plaudits from a wide range of figures, such as Winston Churchill, Sigmund Freud, Mahatma Gandhi, George Bernard Shaw and Thomas Edison. There were even some sensational exploits that occasionally brought the country into the world limelight. In August 1933, the Italian-built luxury ocean liner "Rex" set a new transatlantic record, reaching New York in 4 days, 13 hours and 58 minutes, and was awarded the blue ribbon for speed, which it held till June 1935, when the French "Normandie" beat it. But those were also times of great worldwide interest in aviation, specifically long-distance flight. Earlier the world had acclaimed several milestones. Between 20 May and 7 November 1925 Francesco De Pinedo, a lieutenant colonel in the Italian Royal Navy, on board a Siai S. 16 ter seaplane, with a crew of two, flew 35,000 miles from Italy to Australia to Japan and back again to Italy. On 11 May 1926, Colonel Umberto Nobile, a developer and promoter of semi-rigid airships, left Spitsbergen, Norway, with the Norwegian explorer Roald Amundsen, on board the Italian Navy-built Nobile N-1, re-christened "Norge" (Norway). The airship flew over the Pole and landed two days later in Teller, Alaska. The following year saw the first non-stop solo flight across the Atlantic, from New York to Paris: on 20-21 May 1927, the American pilot Charles Lindbergh, in his Ryan monoplane "Spirit of St. Louis", made it in 33½ hours. These hazardous enterprises relied largely on bold men more than on technological advances likely to render aviation dependable enough for long-distance travel. Lindberg flew a five-passenger plane, normally operating within a much shorter range; its seats had been replaced by extra fuel tanks. Other similarly overloaded challengers crashed in a fire at take-off! A few years later, it was Italo Balbo, who envisaged "mass flying", as he stated in Parliament on 28 March 1928, who led Italian aviation's substantial steps towards commercial transatlantic flights.

Balbo, born in 1896, volunteered at the outbreak of World War I (1915), earned one bronze and two silver medals and was promoted to the rank of captain for his war merits. A graduate in social sciences from Florence University, in the post-war turmoil young Italo baldly joined the ruthless Fascist squads, in his native Emilia region, fighting Socialists and Communist violence and opposing rural strikes and demonstrations. He soon proved a perfect commander and smart organizer; his reputation grew, taking him to the top of the Fascist Party, and he was one of the March on Rome's four leaders (*Quadrumviri*, the others being Michele Bianchi, Emilio De Bono and Cesare De Vecchi).

Mussolini appointed Balbo first of all General Commander of the Militia (1924), a year later Undersecretary to the National Economy, and then Undersecretary to the Air Force (1926). The professor who had supervised Balbo's thesis wrote about his university years: "[They] conferred on him the mental habit which science entails, whereby he never acted as an improviser in any field of his endeavour...". Unlike some Fascist undertakings, flawed by improvisation - most tragically the war itself - Balbo's idea to start a program of group transatlantic flights involved careful study, planning and constant scrutiny. In contrast with previous Italian performances relying on "ordinary" air force personnel, he set up a special flying crew training center in Orbetello (on the Tyrrhenian Sea near Rome), where problems posed by oceanic navigation, radio communication and poor-visibility flying were also tackled.

Meanwhile, leading high-altitude respiratory physiology studies were ongoing in Italy. Rodolfo Margaria, one of the internationally eminent scientists involved, much later taught physiology to Luciano in the Milan University medical school! Several flying squadrons' cruises over the Mediterranean, ordered by Balbo, not only drew international plaudits, but also served to test the progress achieved. Eventually on 17 December 1930, 14 Siai S.55 seaplanes, each fitted with two 600 hp FIAT engines, left Orbetello: Balbo himself, as first pilot of the head plane, led the squadron which crossed the Atlantic and arrived in Rio de Janeiro on 16 January 1931. That aroused extraordinary enthusiasm locally - especially among the many Italian residents - and in the world public opinion. A similarly enthusiastic emotional response to aviation's performances of those times, was seen again only in the last decades of the century, when manned space exploration started.

The next expedition was meant to be unprecedentedly sensational, particularly on account of its destination: the Chicago World Fair of 1933. On 1 July, again led by Balbo, 25 Siai S 55 seaplanes - this

21

time fitted with two 930 hp Isotta Fraschini Asso engines each! - took off from their Italian base to Lake Michigan and New York, for a round trip; the planes returned to Rome on 12 August. Chicago's enthusiastic welcome included renaming Seventh Street "Balbo Drive", staging a parade in his honour and the Sioux's honorary adoption of Balbo as "Chief Flying Eagle". An ancient Roman column, brought there by the expedition as a gift from Mussolini to the city, still stands along the Lakefront Trail, a little south of Soldier Field. The Italian aviators were greeted with the same enthusiasm elsewhere in the USA, especially by the large Italian-American populations, including Luciano's mother's brother John, who had settled there as a first-generation American. President Roosevelt invited Balbo to lunch and presented him with the Distinguished Flying Cross. Besides great world-wide popular fervour, the cruise earned much credit in international aviation technology circles and Balbo's return to Rome was literally a triumph. Mussolini appointed him First *Maresciallo dell'Aria* (Air Force Marshal), Marshal being a title of honour reserved for the generals who contributed to the victory in World War I. As Governor-General of Libya, where he had moved in January 1934, Balbo transformed this backward colony into a model Italian province appealing to immigrants, and attracted substantial numbers of his middle-class compatriots.

Balbo's popularity at home and abroad had no equal: he seemed to embody a noble Fascist vision of the new Italy, but this apparently caused jealousy among many high-ranking Fascists and even Mussolini himself. However, there is controversy about whether he actually disagreed openly with Mussolini, in spite of his irreverent and "individualistic" behaviour, as well as the anglophile, pro-Jewish, anti-German sentiments he never hid: so several legends flourished. The rumour that an order from Mussolini decided Balbo's tragic death by friendly fire in the skies of Tobruk, Libya on 28 June 1940, two weeks after the Italian declaration of war, has been dismissed by solid historical scrutiny.

Luciano's notion of Fascism before War World II evolved from his pre-adolescent perception of the examples of the typical events outlined above, as lived or learned at school, but mostly influenced by his family's background. Such "home conditioning" grew in the conflict years, affecting Luciano's generation and those close to it. Of course it varied considerably depending on the parents' and relatives' standing and fate, sometimes turning into a traumatic experience and even leaving permanent mental scars, especially for the growing boys who suffered the loss of loved ones. Luciano's friend Davide Lajolo, at a certain point in the war - typically in the second half of 1943, when Mussolini was overthrown and arrested by the King, to be rescued shortly thereafter and reinstated by Hitler's Germans who took over northern and most of central Italy - abjured Fascism and fought it in the Resistance forces, whereas Luciano's father Mario continued to side with the soon-to-be-losers. Mario's and Davide's example of two sharply opposing, strongly held beliefs, no matter what hazards were involved, applied to many relatively young adults (under 40 during the war).

Then on 8 September that year they learned that their King had signed an armistice with the Allies which implied siding with them against Germany in a tragic *volte-face*. Confusion reigned; a choice had to be made overnight about which of the opposite sides to join, either along the battle lines or in the hills of northern Italy where the partisan war (the Resistance) caused shameful, fratricidal bloodshed during the last two years of the conflict. In between those deeply divided and often tragically clashing Italians were most others who had never seriously committed themselves to Fascism, nor had they ever really distanced themselves from it. The day the war ended, most had warily deleted any possible evidence of previous siding with Mussolini and many rushed to fabricate longstanding anti-Fascist credentials!

In the second half of the 1940s, when the war was over and the country was home to western Europe's most powerful Soviet-backed Communist Party, generations of Italian school-children started being taught the "winner's" flawed history (the version according to the new left-wing cultural monopoly): allegedly with Fascism's unjustified violence at the roots of its advent to liberticidal power, the oppressed country's hopes of civil and economic growth had vanished for over twenty years. In an excess of Fascist phobia, this teaching carefully avoided mentioning any positive developments in Italy in the 1920s and '30s.

Unquestionably Fascism is to be blamed for everything it did that eventually compelled Italy into the horrors of the war, affecting most of the rest of the world as well. But the records of Italy's achievements in those years can be found, no matter how often under-rated, even in acknowledged historians' harshly critical accounts of every aspect of Fascism, like the ones by the British

Denis Mack Smith. It seems worth recognizing them as examples of a nation's endeavour and creativity, once political stability permitted it, to foster a shared collective memory. Tainting them with the prejudice of Fascism-inspired propaganda, while adopting the Resistance as the latest national myth of patriotic identity, could only further distance "winners" and "losers" and hamper reconciliation.

Several similar issues persisted, mostly unsettled, in Italy into the third millennium, after historians, political scientists and others - mostly domestic - had debated them furiously and at length. The late Renzo de Felice (1929-1996), a former member of the Italian Communist Party who spent most of his life on an all-but-hagiographic, monumental study on Mussolini, was repeatedly accused of writing an apology of Fascism! Eventually, after decades of silence caused by leftish domination of Italian historiography, some successful books have shed light on previously untold stories. The well known journalist and political commentator Gianpaolo Pansa, in his most celebrated (as well as criticized!) book, "*Blood of the Losers*" (2003), followed by two other bestsellers, describes the massacres committed by Communist partisans after 25 April 1945. Antonio Pennacchi was awarded the prestigious *Premio Strega* for his "*Mussolini Canal*" (2010), a historical novel spanning from the beginning of the twentieth century to the aftermath of World War II and centred on the Fascist reclamation of the *Pontine* marshes; unsurprisingly the author was accused of offering an apologetic assessment of Fascism.

After the end of the war, Luciano's father never showed nostalgia for his political past, or sympathized with any neo-Fascist action, and brought up his son Luciano in that spirit. Some time later, though, facing the abuse of the term "Fascist" as a "pejorative epithet" (as George Orwell, the British author of "*Nineteen Eighty-Four*" and "*Animal Farm*" wrote) he sadly recalled his lost hero Italo Balbo!

4. Grandmother Giuseppina

Giuseppina Mensi (1882-1961), Luciano's father's mother, provided a sort of "living memory" of his family's past, the only one dating from the late 19th century; the boy bore its imprint lifelong, having enjoyed a lasting, intense, interaction with her. This was especially so in part of 1939-1940, when grandmother and grandson often lived together alone, since Luciano's parents (and little sister) were away and so was his aunt Cristina (Tina for short), Giuseppina's second child. Grandmother's home in Pietra Marazzi sat on the plain on the south-eastern outskirts of the village, a few miles north-east of Alessandria, one of the main towns of the six provinces of Piedmont. Almost all the dwellings are on the low hill behind; further hills rise in an arch heading from west to north-east. Giuseppina's father, Giuseppe, owned quite a large estate and assigned the western portion to Giuseppina's younger sister Francesca Gillo. She built a house with an ample garden and, while abroad in 1922, let it for a short time to Luciano's future mother Nora's family who were just back from America.

The often quarrelsome sisters' adjacent properties were divided by a row of thick, spiny shrubs about a hundred yards long, which didn't prevent Mario, later to be Luciano's father, and Nora from meeting. On the eastern side of the row of shrubs was Giuseppina's larger portion of her father's former estate, bordered on the south by the main road running east-west, leading to the nearby villages; on its northern edge was the two-hundred-yard eastern section of a village street, Via Novella, merging into the main road. One half of the nearly two-acre triangle-shaped property, where the two sides met at their tip, was a cultivable field. Mulberry trees 40 feet apart rose along its two edges, bordering the roads. The buildings, in a single block, ran alongside the Via Novella, but stood some 10 feet lower so that only the upper floors of the homes had windows opening onto that street. Starting from the border of shrubs, first there was a partly underground basement used as a wine cellar; on top was a terrace with a staircase serving as a pedestrian way out up to Via Novella. Next came the ample two-story house, continuing into a small stable area with a hayloft above it, followed by a broad storehouse also with a hayloft over it. Three huge red brick pillars, each over 10 feet tall, about 15 feet apart, stood facing the storehouse, 30 feet away. The tiled roof of the hayloft above projected forward to form an imposing porch, sustained by those pillars. It faced an orchard alongside the field, stretching to the main road.

On the west side of the orchard was the driveway which ran beside the ample space between the buildings and the main road; there was a courtyard continuing into a garden, and a vegetable garden. Across the road were fields sloping gently down towards the River Tanaro, flowing several hundred yards away. Apparently Luciano was housed by his grandmother in quite a spacious place, which to him at age four seemed even roomier than it actually was. But he never felt scared there - except at night in the really big room upstairs where he slept alone; no matter that both its doors opened onto grandmother's bedroom - it was the same size as the impressive ground floor dining room! The little boy had a lot to explore and discover.

Giuseppina's surname was common in the village but her grandson learned that she was actually related to only a few of these Mensi families. After she left school to take care of her two younger sisters, when their mother died (Cristina Avezza, shown as a charming young lady in an impressively large portrait in the dining room), Giuseppina's father's brother, a priest, Don Matteo, helped her with further education. Grandmother was one of the few people in the village - probably the only woman - who regularly read a newspaper. Giuseppina was proud of (and most grateful to) a Mensi relative, presumably a second cousin, who served the Royal Family in Turin as pediatrician; he saved Luciano's future father's brain from permanent damage - and possibly saved his life in fact. Giuseppina's infant son had a worryingly high fever when the genial early-20th-century physician rushed to his rescue which, to the bystanders' astonishment, consisted in plunging the ailing creature into a basin full of melting snow - just in time to prevent convulsions! Luciano too felt a special kind of gratitude to this doctor he never met, when, two decades later, in a medical school exam, he cited the episode as a pioneer example of lowering body temperature (hypothermia) for therapeutic purposes: he earned top marks!

A native of Pietra Marazzi, Giuseppina had moved to the nearby city of Tortona prior to Italy's involvement in World War I (1915-1918), when she married Carlo Manara, a wealthy local entrepreneur whose business included wine trade, a commercial laundry servicing the army, brick kilns and more. Luciano never found out what kind of education grandfather Carlo had received - he only met him shortly before his death in 1959 - but still has part of his library consisting of technical manuals concerning his affairs, and some wine testing tools. Amongst other items, there is also his shotgun (a 12-gauge double-barrel 19th-century hammer-type gun, skilfully restored after it was recovered from the well where Giuseppina had dumped it as World War II arrived - she was scared of getting into trouble for owning that firearm). Carlo's business started to fail in the aftermath of the first world conflict; he went bankrupt, left the country and joined his brother Mario in Argentina, where he remained, only coming back briefly to Italy, where he died. Giuseppina, who had lost everything in Tortona, resettled in her ancestors' estate in Pietramazzi, and managed to raise her teenage son and daughter by letting part of it, with the land she owned. Tina became a kindergarten teacher (and later a voluntary Red Cross nurse); Mario got a diploma as *"ragioniere"* (accountant), enrolled in the Turin University school of economics and was offered a good job in a bank. However, having witnessed the post-WWI Communist raids in Tortona, and blaming them for his father's business going bust, he couldn't resist Mussolini's bold movement's appeal and, to join it, in the early 1920s he gave up his tranquil job at the bank and the further fun of a students' life in Turin.

To Luciano, or anybody else, the best view from grandmother's estate was the fairly close, high hill hiding Montecastello, a medieval burg built on its north-east-facing far slope. The castle topping that hill enchanted and puzzled the boy when he first spotted it; the unusual edifice had largely been restored (probably in the late 18th century) and stood, palace-like, around its oddly fitting, quite tall square tower raised in the Middle Ages, possibly on the remains of some imperial Roman structure. The castle's glamorous days must have been in the 1500s when it was part of the domain of the Marquises Stampa whose forefather Maximilian was a vassal of Francis II Sforza, the last duke of Milan. Generally castles engender legends and there was of course one centred on Pietra Marazzi. Alessandro Manzoni's *"Promessi Sposi"*(The Betrothed), the 19th-century poet and novelist's masterpiece, portrays the struggle of two peasant lovers who want to marry in 17th-century Lombardy during the anti-Spanish insurrection and the plague. It begins with a bullying scene, while still holding patriotic appeal to the author's contemporary Italians, in view of the future nation's *Risorgimento*. A vicious local tyrant had sent several of his people (in the second millennium we might call them body guards) to tell the cowardly priest who was supposed to marry the betrothed that he shouldn't. There were always murmurs about Mr. Garrone, the bully who owned the castle overlooking Pietra Marazzi in the late 19th century. It appears that he didn't bother to send body guards - if he had any - because of his fancy for any bride but "simply" raped young peasant women working in the nearby fields. It is not clear why none of them ever bothered to accuse him, while many continued, undeterred, venturing alone in the castle's surroundings!

Giuseppina, of course, didn't deem such gossip suitable for recounting to her grandson, but much amused him with accounts deserving better credit and whose central character was Mr. Garrone's somewhat younger widow Jole, around the late 1920s. Grandmother described her as always wearing a wig to hide her ears, which had been mutilated by leprosy. Jole used to give parties attended mostly by locals, preferably handsome, educated and smart youths like Luciano's father's best friend Aldo Ravasi, a notary, and the Italian national soccer player Giuseppe Fenoglio, whose younger sister Ada Luciano would have met as his kindergarten teacher. Those entertainments featured dancing to the rhythms of the day, provided by a player piano. Similar instruments, otherwise identical to a regular piano, included a device that pumped a stream of air through cardboard rolls perforated to reproduce the sequence of notes in the music to activate hammers striking the strings.

Many years later Luciano, as a lifelong friend of Giorgio Bolgeo who then owned the castle, discovered that long-neglected peculiar instrument and a roll of "*Maple Leaf Rag*", a popular ragtime tune by the black American composer and pianist of the turn of the 20th century, Scott Joplin; regrettably, none of several efforts by the two friends to play that and other rolls again, were successful.

At her parties Jole used to serve champagne which, the guests reported, was presented in basins full of snow, regardless of the season, apparently because the castle's cellars, carved deeply into the hill, could preserve plenty of it unmelted. Jole's social life, however, was by no means limited to that hospitality. She loved horses (and riders even more!) and attended competitive equestrian events, particularly jumping. There she fell in love with a much younger, talented horseman of the Royal Army cavalry (according to Giuseppina he was in his twenties and she over sixty) and they married. They retired to the castle and right away, to the dismay of the former guests, parties were over. But somebody else was ready to offer them a special wild one. Were the culprits those Jole had invited to the castle before? Was it a token of scorn by peasants grumbling at that odd marriage? The very night of the wedding, a herd of mongrel dogs each carefully fitted with a tin pan tied to its tail, and a similar score of cats, were sneakily brought into the castle park (through different openings) and freed there!

Grandmother was a gifted storyteller and Luciano, like all the boys of his age at the time, was accustomed and receptive to stories he was told, rather than to then non-existent TV cartoons and the like; the boy closed his eyes and felt, as if he were on the spot on a moonless night, he could hear the barking of the poor scared dogs and all the inferno they raised, together with the no less abused, troubled cats. The happy times of the castle were over; shortly afterwards Jole was found shot dead, with her husband's pistol nearby: the *carabinieri* (the King's police) arrested him. To the man's relief, however, Jole's farewell letter which freed her husband from that nightmare didn't stay long undisclosed.

Other stories by Giuseppina generally involved family members or relatives Luciano never met. There was her sister-in-law Gemma's husband Mr. Casalegno, a former *carabiniere* who lost his life when, unarmed, he boldly resisted the demands of Sante Polastri, a pugnacious Piedmont bandit of the first decades of the 20th century, who wanted the money he was carrying on behalf of a bank. A dramatic full-page color picture of the onslaught, signed by Achille Beltrame, appeared on the front cover of the weekly magazine *La Domenica del Corriere* published by the leading Italian newspaper *Il Corriere della Sera*. Beltrame, Italy's most celebrated illustrator in the first half of the 20th century, published most of the similar pages devoted to sensational current events, from the paper's foundation in 1899 until 1945. Much later on, in the 1990s, Luciano's search for the issue of that magazine in which Beltrame honored Mr. Casalegno as a civil hero was unsuccessful; oddly enough, however, on extending the search to the *Corriere della Sera*, Luciano spotted (in its issue of 1 June 1991) news of the indictment of Giorgio Casalegno, the civil hero's grandson, a top financial manager involved in an international organized crime gang!

The story of Paolo Orecchia, another relative of Giuseppina's who Luciano occasionally met because he was a close friend of his father, offered an example of how a life-threatening accident may turn into a stroke of luck. Paolo, as a little boy around 1910 in Castello d'Annone, a village on the southern section of the national highway connecting Turin, the regional capital of Piedmont, with Alessandria, was playing when a rare passing automobile hit him and made the residents furious. Regardless of whether or not he himself had been driving that car, Senator Giovanni Agnelli, the boss of FIAT, the largest Italian automobile manufacturer, not only supported the rescued boy till he got his university degree in mechanical engineering, but granted him Turin's number one FIAT dealership (with protectionism, FIAT enjoyed a virtual monopoly on car sales, and its dealers in each town ranked socially not much lower than the bishop!).

Generally grandmother told Luciano these tales and others like them in the kitchen while sitting in front of the huge fireplace whose red bricks inside had turned charcoal black. Most of the times the black cat Majno sat there as well, named after the legendary local robber backed by the populace as a rebel to Napoleon's oppressive rule in the early 1800s. Grandmother's Majno too was an impenitent thief and enjoyed a good share of the fine cuts of beef Giuseppina bought for her grandson. The kitchen was also where his grandmother sang opera music while doing the dishes or similar chores; occasionally she would turn on the radio, which was just beside the door in the adjacent dining room, when it broadcast opera. Luciano had a good ear for picking up those sounds and soon started to sing himself, to her delight. Throughout his life, though, Luciano was never a fan of that kind of vocal music, nor did he attend opera performances, though he liked some overtures and symphonies. However, each time he happened to listen accidentally to arias from "Trovatore", "Boheme", "Traviata" and the like, he had that sense of déjà vu (perhaps better déjà écouté !) and he could have sung along as he used to do with his grandmother.

Because of the slow development of his brain after birth, a young human's ability to distinguish, recognize, memorize and, specifically, reproduce sounds, grows to a maximum before puberty and then declines sharply (as attested by one's inability to speak impeccably a language learnt later on in life). Thus that sort of informal introduction to music, thanks to Giuseppina, could not but benefit Luciano's future enjoyment of listening to all the forms he was interested in. Hearing can be enriched by proper "priming-training" in the formative years - or irreversibly damaged, for instance by prolonged exposure to strong acoustic stimuli, like when misusing earphones. While learning all these stories and more from his grandmother, Luciano seldom stayed silent long; his curiosity was usually excited by many details in the accounts, no matter if marginal, and he couldn't refrain from putting questions, over and over again. No doubt Giuseppina was a bit upset by those interruptions but always gave her best possible answers. Of course she loved her little grandson and should be forgiven for claiming he was a genius. Mind you, Luciano had a sharp recollection of that and of asking what the word meant. Most probably grandmother's exaggeration reflected her experience with children of similar ages, generally from among the lower-class people of the village, including those she had let part of her house to in the past. At that time, though, Luciano had had much less contact with his peers than with adults, with whom he felt more at ease when he first met them, and was unusually outspoken too; that presumably impressed them. However, child development (according to scholars of our own day - in the second millennium) closely depends on peer-group experience; this, and further occurrences, may explain why Luciano, possibly fairly bright for his age at four, slowed down worryingly in the first year of primary school.

Outdoor activities with grandmother also offered the lad plenty of opportunities for asking and learning: field-learning from first-hand observation was of special value. Tomato plants live just for one year and must be planted afresh the next one; some huge trees, like oaks, also grow from a seed, but outlive men; herbs may be friendly like parsley, or deadly like the water-hemlock that resembles it (the plant used to kill Socrates, according to tradition); hens lay eggs, cocks don't, but they crow. Giuseppina had a few hens and when she wanted to pick one up and check whether it was about to lay, the bird would willingly sit still and let her do so. Yet the fowls never trusted Luciano, who chased them, upsetting the vicious cock, and risking being pecked. However, the boy did become a successful egg seeker (the hens roamed freely in Giuseppina's estate and would lay their eggs anywhere).

One of grandmother and grandson's almost-daily walks took them up the hill to where she owned a small vineyard and some land. Only a few hard tracks that climbed the hills straight up to the top were wide enough for oxen-drawn carts to cross on their way up or down, while the narrower side-trails led to generally small individual plots, often hardly an acre, where their owners grew either cereals or grass for forage, or laid them as vineyards. Trees, mostly oaks, rose along the roadsides and trails; thus from a distance the hills, typically in that region, looked as though they were covered with a cloth made like an uneven patchwork, whose gently shifting seasonal colors changed year-round, the tracks and trails somehow standing out as green or dark brown ribbons depending on the season.

South-eastward across the river, as seen from the hills overlooking the village, was the plain with only a few large farms, homes of wealthy owners. In clear weather, the peaks of the Apennine Mountains rose to the horizon. On his way back from the hills Luciano used to take home some "souvenirs" like acorns, the nuts of the oak trees. He had played with them in grandmother's vegetable garden, and one or two years later she showed him a seedling with a few oak-like leaves: he decided that was meant to be his tree. Each time he returned to the village after staying somewhere else, he would go to check whether his future majestic oak was coming up all right; it was already taller than him when he was not yet ten!

In the next half of the century Pietra Marazzi enjoyed progress, with an aqueduct and sewers. Its west-to-north-east three hills had been "distorted": two by newcomers' oddly-fitting modern houses, the third by the fact that most once-small vineyards and differently cultivated plots had been transformed into a vast treeless area accessible to big motorized farming machines. No more oaks rose alongside the widened, paved roads travelled mostly by SUVs. One huge, towering tree, though, dropped acorns and shaded a good deal of the late Giusppina's estate, made substantially more comfortable, but preserving its look virtually unchanged; in the field, wheat or corn, both so appreciated in times of food shortage during the war, were replaced by a well watered and manicured lawn.

 As grandmother – and Luciano's father too – had taught him, her estate in the village where he had been making his rural and other discoveries since age three and four, had offered them and aunt Tina shelter earlier in the 20th century, when the failure of the family head's business in nearby Tortona had unexpectedly caused their former comfortable lifestyle to come to a sudden end. Luciano himself witnessed throughout World War II the value of that estate as a blessed shelter from much of the coming distress. But when the war was over and the time came to forget and look ahead, the grown boy's memories of grandmother's refuge faded and so did many others tying him to that site: there was a lot more he needed to discover.

Nevertheless, much later in life, Giuseppina's grandson, having long chased his dreams and struggled with his fate, mostly far away in distant places, began to turn back to his early years in old house in the village, where he felt more and more that he belonged. Then, no matter if only to sleep there one night because of his appointments, as an adult he eagerly grasped any opportunity to return to Pietra Marazzi, which felt like a life-giving breath of fresh air: a sort of "momentary break away from over-civilization!" in his own words. Just the sight of the castle tower in the distance would allow him relaxing thoughts. When on a plane approaching one of the two principal airports of the Lombardy region, both a little over one hour's drive from Pietra Marazzi, he had figured out how to spot the tower, by looking first for the River Tanaro.

Further on, he managed to make his stays there a little longer, just to get involved with planting new fruit trees or the like; he also realized there was a "family museum" including his racing motorbike of the 1950s, his father's last car (an Alfa Romeo of the '60s), his grandfather's antique shotgun, Giuseppina's first radio and much else. Each one of those objects evoked more than one story!

In essence, having lived through most of his odyssey, eventually Luciano, like Homer's wandering hero Ulysses, told himself: "Nowhere in the world is there any place sweeter than home". The boy of yore, now well over seventy, retired to his virtually native countryside. He largely curbed his long- standing former professional interests to a meagre stay-in-touch, trying hard to read and study. Otherwise as far as he could he started to dig into his father's archives and, lucky enough to be fit, took care of the garden, vegetable garden, lawns and trees, as he had learned.

One night, grey-haired Luciano had a dream borrowed from a short autobiographic account by José Saramago. It was he, not the1998 Nobel Laureate's old father, setting out first to say goodbye to each of his trees, before being taken to hospital, from where he knew would have never come back home. Luciano woke up while struggling with his most loved oak: it was too big to embrace!

5. In the Heart of the Dolomites

The Dolomites, a spectacular mountain range boasting a number of impressive peaks, quite a few rising to more than 10,000 ft, shape the eastern section of the Italian Alps, in the Veneto region. The rocks take their name from the 18th-century French geologist Dieudonné Dolomieu, who first explored the area. The vast cliffs forming one of the most beautiful mountain landscapes anywhere are made of a peculiar variety of light-colored limestone, which erosion carves into unusual, evocative forms, often reminding us of humans, animals or objects. The attractive lower landforms are scree slopes, patches of woodland - once forests - grassy meadows and a few small lakes. The United Nations Educational, Scientific and Cultural Organization (UNESCO) has included the Dolomites on the World Heritage List. On the foothills 50 miles north of Venice sits the town of Belluno, bounded on the south by the River Piave, where Luciano spent about two years, part of 1941, 1942 and the first half of 1943, and did his first two years of primary school. The Dolomites, closely looming over the city, offer a scenic skyline to Belluno (elevation 1,300 ft), the head town of one of the Veneto region's provinces, a beautiful, quiet, clean, friendly, small township with its own micro-climate, protected by the mountains and enviably pollution-free. Founded by the Romans in the last two centuries BC, Belluno became part of Venice in late medieval Europe, one of the four Maritime Republics of that epoch (with Amalfi, Genoa and Pisa), and an important hub for delivering lumber for shipyards and construction, via the River Piave. In those years, however, Luciano learned only a much less remote story about the river, as told in the patriotic *Canzone del Piave* (Piave Song) he was taught at school. In World War I the Piave became the main Italian line of defence after the Austrians' breakthrough turned into the Caporetto rout; eventually they were decisively defeated at the Battle of Vittorio Veneto at the end of October 1918.

Luciano retained recollections of many scattered episodes, most of them trivial, in Belluno. Some surfaced in his adulthood, surprisingly triggered by apparently unrelated later events. Early in 1941 his family first settled on the town outskirts, occupying part of a house they shared with its owners. Mesdames Smaniotto, mother and daughter, were both distinguished, black-dressed widows, occasionally smoking little eye-watering cigars; they lived with two teenage girls, the daughters of the younger widow. All loved to pet the little lad, but refrained from kissing his cheeks (he hated that - when less thoughtful old ladies kissed him, Luciano would promptly wipe off the "smear" with his forearm and frown!).

The main view, quite close from the apartment's rear windows, was an odd one, especially when first seen - it was the cemetery! Next to his home, which faced the road leading to the nearby town of Feltre, was an elusive mansion, hidden by high walls all around its park. The owner's surname, *Terribile* ("Terrible"), could be seen on the gate; the boy, though, could not read at the time but was told about it by the older lads in the neighbourhood. He joined them one evening in a sort of witch-play: they boiled their catch of unlucky tadpoles! The boy not yet six-year-old when he got to Belluno, saved no memory of attending kindergarten there or anywhere (except a short stint in Pietra) previously. His lack of any other recollection about kindergarten (usually significant for children of that age) is hardly accounted for by scarce attendance because of poor health; it is puzzling that he recalls so many other contemporary details. According to some, the very act of recalling things or events (rehearsal) keeps memories permanent; they tend to be forgotten if they are not "reactivated" from time to time. Forgetting can also function as a protective measure against potential anxiety elicited by rehearsing unpleasant experiences: had something unpleasant happened to the boy in kindergarten? Yet Luciano didn't erase his brain's encoding (the biochemical substrate of memories sought by neuroscientists in the third millennium) of childhood illnesses. When he caught whooping cough, things got worse, purportedly due to failure to give him a series of five intramuscular injections as "challenges", in the order the doctor had prescribed. The poor kid was kept in bed for weeks, but got anything he asked for by his adoring, caring mother - possibly even a small revolver which he had spotted in the drawer of a night table in his parents' bedroom. The poor woman struggled first to divert Luciano's attention to something else - like her own first-Communion gift, a set of earrings consisting of two

1910 gold Indian-head two-and-a-half US dollar coins which he had always loved to play with. Mom's unsuccessful efforts ended with a sort of goofy safety check of that weapon. Having never had to deal with a firearm, she decided to fire a shot out of the window, and was relieved when there was just one click. So she handed that potentially fatal "toy" to her son with a relaxed smile! However, thanks to Luciano's father's safe habit of hiding his ammunition far from the handguns he kept unloaded, there was no real risk of deadly "Russian roulette". For a later problem, Luciano needed minor surgery it turned out to be a bit stressful because of the "primitive" general anesthesia in those years. A swab soaked with ethyl ether was pressed onto his face: for a short while he felt lousy, but then he started to see the most beautiful colors of his life exploding like fireworks in a magic kaleidoscope. Coming round was the worst part, with pain, vomiting, and fright. The boy never forgot being carried up a staircase by a nun in a white habit, screaming his lungs out! That was what the specialists dub a flashbulb memory, an indelible engram of a unique, highly emotional moment.

Luciano's early World War II times in Belluno had nothing to do with the battlefields all around the city dating from the first world conflict. Life a quarter of a century later looked as quiet and serene in many ways as in the previous few years. Several substantial changes though, had taken place. Quite a few young men had had to leave their loved ones worrying at home, wearing an armed forces' uniform somewhere far away. One man meant to leave too in the incoming year was Luciano's father. Of course, only later on, as an adult, did he truly realize how the apparently thriving world he had experienced as a little boy turned into the tragic downfall of the conflict.
The country's sorry fate had been decided on 10 June 1940, with Mussolini's disgraceful declaration of war on France and England. The *Duce* was disgruntled with the events of the German-driven war not having been disclosed to him in advance, like annexing Austria in March 1938 and, mainly, the agreement with Russia of August '39; this was the Ribbentrop-Molotov pact, so dubbed after the German and Russian foreign ministers names who were secretly working out how to share Poland's territories once invaded: it preluded the Soviet aggression on Finland by the end of the year. This latter hostile act was badly received by Italian public opinion and students demonstrated furiously, an unprecedented event in those times. Mussolini struggled to make the most of Hitler's assertive politics,

without getting involved as his active battle ally, in spite of "The Pact of Steel" Italy signed with Germany in May 1939, without insisting that it would be exclusively defensive!

On 28 September 1938, Hitler was setting out to invade Czechoslovakia, a protégé of France, but Mussolini managed to stop him and held a conference in Munich where on the 30th he got England, France and Germany to agree they would negotiate a solution for the German population of Czech territories. That apparently stood out as a successful example of Mussolini's potential European appeasing role, which several figures like Pope Pius XII and the U.S. president F. D. Roosevelt had encouraged, in view of the *Duce's* special relationship with Hitler. However, the three powers in Munich had only agreed to postpone the war, as they wanted time to get ready for it better. On the other hand, Italy's "friendly" annexing of Albania in April 1939 was at odds with Mussolini's cautious maneuvering (although the international community didn't complain). On 25 August 1939 Great Britain and Poland signed a treaty of mutual assistance; on the 31st Hitler started to invade Poland; on 3 September Great Britain and France declared war on Germany - World War II had begun. Italy stayed neutral, but further events of 1940 set the *Duce* a conundrum where he seemed to be flip-flopping between keeping out of the war and siding with Hitler. Early in the year the British had started a naval block of the Mediterranean Sea; the Germans invaded Norway and Denmark on 9 April and France on 10 May, passing through Holland and Belgium. With these sudden irresistible advances and conquests by the German armies, Mussolini stopped wavering, in the belief that the hostilities wouldn't last long, and he would risk taking sides too late. He also feared - like so many of his men, as well as a growing proportion of pro-war public opinion, similarly impressed by the initial defeats of the anti-Hitler coalition - that a betrayed German ally would sooner or later turn against Italy. It didn't help a last diplomatic efforts by England, France, and the U.S.A. to dissuade him from joining Hitler's armed forces, as well the Duce's belated understanding that Italy was ill-prepared to go to war: Mussolini took the country into the greatest and deadliest conflict of its history (40-50 million deaths!), leading to wide-scale ruin.

The Germans reached Paris on 14 June and on the 17th the French government asked for an armistice which cut short Italy's initial attack on the French Alps. Meanwhile, in the very days after Mussolini's declaration of war (10 June), British Royal Air Force planes based in the South of France raided Turin and Genoa; the latter city also suffered   bombardment by the French Mediterranean fleet. Those strikes which caused civilian casualties were only an early warning, hardly representative of the "carpet bombings" which, in the coming years, would cruelly ravage unarmed populations far from the battlegrounds, throughout most of the world.

Obviously young Luciano had only vague notions of the war going on, nor could he perceive any of the daily horrors. So he carried on playing the favorite games of kids of his age at the time, maneuvering all sort of toys like guns, tanks, bombers, warships, and other military tricks. Wasn't that a sort of innocent, but sardonic mockery of the real cruel conflict? Anthropologists maintain that war games are one of the first things taught to the young in many human cultures; it probably developed from the instinct for self-preservation - a natural club or stick was the prototype of toy swords. Still, the military toys boys played with during the second world conflict, while generally crafted to give a fairly accurate imitation of the real things, could not of course convey any idea of their deadly potential and the cruelty they caused. The little warriors were still unaware that war is evil! In the 21st century, that kind of toys are mostly collectors' items and - wisely enough - seem no longer to be promoted so hard for youngsters. In the developed world, boys seem to prefer to play star wars with funny-looking fantastic weapons, only remotely related to today's real military firearms which, sadly, are still handled by some of their unlucky peers, child soldiers in the poorest troubled regions of the planet.

Luciano's war game memories in Belluno took two forms. When he was alone he would lay out practically all his military toys on the floor like on a battleground and move them around to simulate actions such as assaults, bombing, and taking prisoners. Luciano's pal Enzo Rubino, a couple of years older, who lived in the apartment next door on the same floor in the downtown building where Luciano's family had settled, offered a different option: the two boys played combat troops. Their main equipment consisted of much-loved toy firearms making noisy bursts and enough smoke that the boys' furious battles ended with Luciano's mother opening all the windows. Luciano and Enzo never shot each other - How could friends do that ? Who would agree to play the part of the hated enemy? The boys, either lying on the floor or taking cover behind an armchair or the like, just aimed their weapons at the same invisible foe.

Luciano had no doubt that the vicious foe was around, since Enzo (who unlike him could already read fluently) had explained the meaning of a slogan painted in man-size letters on the windowless side of a nearby building: "Keep quiet: the enemy can overhear you!". Other painted phrases were common around town; one read: "Butter or cannons?" and Mum's explanation to Luciano was that, because of the war, people had to adapt to the lack of many items, including certain foods. Accordingly, each household, depending on the number and age of its members, was given ration stamps they could use to buy a given amount of specific items. Trading those items – on the black market – was, of course, illegal and entailed imprisonment for selling them and a fine to the buyer. Other slogans on the walls of buildings were followed by a stylized "M" (to show they were Mussolini's own words). One of the best known was: "It's better to live one day as a lion, than a hundred years as a sheep".

Luciano has several fairly clear reminiscences of downtown Belluno during his boyhood there, starting (then he was six) with the apartment building which became his second home there.
The flat his family rented on the second floor consisted of a row of spacious rooms from kitchen to bathroom, all the same width and differing only in their length. The windows were all on the same side, at the rear of the house looking south and facing an ample courtyard. The entrance was on the other side, leading straight into the living room. The walls between the rooms all ended with a door, at right angles to the wall with the windows. Built into a niche in the windowed wall beside each door, there was a "Cadorine" stove (from Cadore, a north-eastern Veneto district comprising the upper River Piave basin). Those heaters were a real blessing in the long chilly winters of the region. They were designed to retain heat by channelling the smoke and hot air from the fire through a labyrinth of pipes.
Besides Enzo and his family, other neighbours, the Coronas (they might have been the landlords?) lived downstairs on the first floor. Luciano had first tried to get noticed by Marlisa, their daughter, presumably just into her early teens, by dropping a few stamps from his collection (whether his parents approved we shall never know!) from a window overlooking the courtyard and a terrace where she played. Luciano used to join Marlisa downstairs and enjoyed listening to her stories, either those she had read in books, or "non-fiction" accounts on any old topic. The girl wore dental braces which didn't spoil her frequent enticing smiles, at least in the boy's eyes.

She had a brother, a bit older, always in a wheelchair. Luciano had seen him once riding a tandem bicycle with his mother and occasionally liked to chat to him too. He was curious about the boy's disability: one of his legs looked disproportionately underdeveloped and he asked silly, probably childish questions, including whether that skinny leg would ever catch up with the other. The disabled youth was really nice and would reassure his worried little rubbernecker that he would certainly eventually get better. Only two decades later, thanks to Albert Sabin and Jonas Salk, mass polio vaccination became available and Luciano, then just out of medical school, sadly recalled Marlisa's crippled brother and his well-intentioned fib.

A further puzzling experience involving memory mechanisms arose when one day Marlisa, without saying anything, surprised Luciano by taking his hand and sliding it onto her lap so he could feel a safety pin which secured a homemade pad of the type used in those days for women's cycles. The boy hadn't the slightest idea what that was all about so it was completely meaningless to him and he didn't even ask, nor did the girl provide any clue.

Oddly enough, though, the obscure happening, which hardly interested Luciano at the time and sank deep down into his memory right away, resurfaced sharp and no longer mysterious when he was a medical student. In neurophysiology, he learned about stereognosis (tactile recognition), the ability to recognize objects by touch without looking at them. Marlisa, whom he had never met or heard of again, came back to mind with an affectionate feeling for a little girl proud to confirm that she was now a woman!

On the ground floor at the front of the building facing one of the main streets (named after some obscure "celebrity" called Gerolamo Segato) there was the main entrance (number 19, an odd number like all the other buildings on that side) and several windows of Mr. Dadalt's liquor store; he lived in an apartment somewhere on the upper floors. Mr. Dadalt, a tall, portly man, had certain special wartime duties concerning the building and its residents, such as making sure that no light filtered out at night through properly darkened windows; that gas masks were available for every resident; that in case of alarm everybody would join him in the basement set up as an air raid shelter. Across the street there was an edifice where Luciano's father had his office; it stood out as a typical, unmistakable example of Fascist architecture, thoughtlessly torn down in 1982 to build the odd looking Court offices!

The ample courtyard at the rear of Luciano's home, had lower buildings on both sides and a gate opening onto another street: there were some small businesses often busy in the daytime. The main one was a car repair shop (belonging to the Coronas), and to Luciano's delight he was allowed to watch the machinists at work on trucks in the yard. Two of those men had the same Christian name, Luigi; little Luigi - the other was a sort of giant – was wonderfully patient in answering the boy's countless questions. The others nicknamed him "pincin", meaning small in the Venetian dialect, a colorful language used in some of the plays written by Carlo Goldoni, the acclaimed renovator of the Italian *commedia dell'arte* in the 1700s.

Most of the locals in Belluno usually spoke Venetian and Luciano ended up understanding some of it but, strangely enough, he hardly remembers a word of that dialect other than *sghei* (money), and in fact claims he has never had any interest in it at any time in his life! At Mom's insistence Luciano had memorized his home address in Belluno (she let him go out on his own for short walks - the place was absolutely safe), but he never had any occasion later in life to recall the street name. It must have been meant to fall into oblivion until he visited the University of Florence and its Human Anatomy Museum. There he finally became acquainted with Gerolamo Segato from Belluno, a controversial 19th-century naturalist, known for his ability to perfectly preserve corpses, by "petrifying" them with a procedure whose secret he took with him to his grave. The naturalist's name surfaced, from the depths of Luciano's early memories, as the street where he had lived in Belluno; at least in this case it seems that rehearsal had not been necessary!

6. Growing up in Belluno

   Luciano was not yet six when he arrived and almost eight when he left Belluno, but was mature enough - through various "experiences" including a strictly platonic "love affair" and one only slightly less so! - to become increasingly aware of the emotional states, typical of that age. Of course he had no idea of how his evolving brain accounted for this psychological development, and in fact he would have liked to learn about it, even if only grossly, much later on in life.

Unlike most other mammals whose development is already fairly advanced at birth, so they are soon no longer in need of adults' care (as a striking exception sperm whales apparently suckle their young for over ten years), human newborns are to a far greater extent wonderfully complex, delicate, living "projects" that need long-term nesting in a protected habitat; each one will eventually grow into a different mature individual, normally a healthy John (or Joan) Doe. Yet examples like Alexander of Macedonia and Catherine of Russia, both referred to as "The Great", suggest how far one can in fact grow up, however uncommon it may be!

Scientific advances in the second half of the 20th century have given us new assurance that a lot is already "written" in our inborn blueprints although the environment decisively affects them too, helping shape the outcome of those plans. "Nature" (our genes) is interwoven with "nurture" (our environment). While slower in reaching their full development, humans are by no means stronger than many other mammals. However, man's brain has evolved unbelievably more than in any other species, so Homo sapiens has cut himself a niche as the smartest - the dominant one. Neuroscientists tell us that the number of specialized cells (neurons) in our brain at birth is astonishing - around one hundred billion just in the "noblest" part, the cortex, rivalling the number of stars in our galaxy! - and remains the same throughout life, though the human brain stops growing at puberty. A major step in this development - and later on - is when the neurons start connecting to each other; this results in an average of ten thousand connections (synapses) per neuron, which in turn implies a potential of a trillion synapses! Neuroscientists add that these "infinite" networks not only govern all our body functions, but are also the site of sensations, emotions, thoughts and the like that go to make up the individuality and identity of a person: his self, as he perceives it. While the genetic makeup alone initially (even before birth) shapes the neuronal networks, experience and events prevail later in life and their influence never ends. Experience, however, is vital for attaining specific physical or mental skills in the formative years of adolescence, when personality traits are also influenced most.

Luciano's experience in Belluno no doubt had significant effects on the neurobiological substrate of his developing personality. Two of the most significant events of those years were entering primary school and getting ready for the Christian sacrament of Communion. An unforeseen occurrence was his father leaving home in the summer of 1942 to join the Italian army on the Russian front. All that added up to a real challenge for the growing boy and left its mark on his mind unlike any past event or state. Until then he had not had any major obligations other than obeying his parents or the close relatives who looked after him. Luciano's previous social interactions inside and outside the home only involved close family friends and were always agreeable. His experience with his peers had also always been friendly: that had been mostly in the countryside around Pietra Marazzi village, where the little local kids, generally from families of modest socio-cultural conditions, welcomed the exuberant imaginative newcomer and often allowed him a dominant role in their games. Luciano had some health problems before school opened, so he started classes late - presumably well over a month late - and he was not given homework to help make up for the time lost. The *Aristide Gabelli* public primary school (named after a 19th-century educationist) was one of Belluno's civic boasts: there were several examples of fine contemporary architecture. The school buildings had impressively ample windows, were surrounded by gardens and playgrounds, in a vast fenced area with lawns and trees; pupils wore smocks, white for girls and black for boys. The latecomer liked the place, but much less most of the people there, except for three whose lasting memory he jealously saved: his much-loved teacher, the charming lady who taught music once a week and his school pal Marisa. The boy never really overcome the main problem of "fitting in":

44

the pupils he joined had already got to know each other and the social and learning aspects of their new experience. They were healthy and lively, while he was still frail for occasional long periods. Possibly his origin didn't help either. Luciano's school pals all spoke with the sing-song Venetian accent, quite different from his own, which revealed the French influence in Piedmont's dialect. In summary, the late arrival in the class often felt like an insecure alien from the very start, being much less curious and eager to live his first year in school than his contemporaries. And things soon went from bad to worse.

Luciano never forgot his teacher, Mrs. Ciabattoni, who used to be just as dedicated to her pupils as to her six children; she was his saving angel throughout his troubled first year in primary school. The lovely lady of course had immediately noted Luciano's troublesome learning gap and patiently encouraged him, as she would have done anyway for those left behind, though in his class none of the others had problems. The boy found certain tasks hard to cope with, like handling the pens of those days, which needed an inkstand! His hand shook hopelessly all the time.

For a while the arrangements were that boys and girls each had their own little desk and the teacher checked what they had done without the others necessarily knowing the result. So Luciano's poor performance was hardly apparent to the rest of the class; one day, however, it showed up embarrassingly. That recollection is blurred but its persistence, like that of any disagreeable experience, was most probably subject to efforts at removal, or *repression* as psychiatrists call it. It must have been a class exercise in which each pupil had to do much the same thing, presumably a kind of reading/spelling contest. Sure enough, when it came to Luciano's turn, his funny mistake prompted sudden howls of laughter around the classroom! Looking back, we would have no doubt that it was nothing more than an innocent, joyful expression of his classmates' amusement, but the unlucky performer felt they were laughing at him and was "struck dumb", feeling it was a display of scorn. Mrs. Ciabattoni rushed to the rescue with support, and from then on she stayed even closer to the boy; that same day she asked Marisa to hand him a set of her colour pencils as a "consolation present".

Marisa, the brightest pupil, tall, black-haired, deep brown eyes, serious, sat in the first row, spoke only to the teacher when asked, never smiled, and didn't look haughty at all - if anything she seemed a bit shy. To Luciano the girl had been like a vision ever since he had

first seen her; he admired her proficiency, but there was also something magic about her, something he had never felt before. Sadly that sort of angelic view was also a bit stunning, even more so because the enchanted boy, after his recent setbacks in class, was no longer anything like as openhearted and self-confident as the lad who had so successfully befriended his peers in Pietra Marazzi.
In that frame of mind, he couldn't even bring himself to mutter a word of thanks to the girl for the pencils and after missing that chance never dared take another opportunity to say anything to her. Later on though, sometimes he felt bold enough to look briefly into her eyes (deeply?) and she wouldn't turn or walk away, like she did when other pals approached her. Whether Marisa ever graced Luciano with a hint of a smile will never be known!

Attending school was therefore a pretty discouraging, barely profitable endeavour for Luciano, though not only and not always. In his daily struggle he soon realized that Mrs. Ciabattoni was a formidable ally who cared about him. He was grateful, admiring her and was relieved to understand that somebody wanted to help him. A striking example of the lady's laudable attention to her pupils' appearance was when she noticed her protégé didn't walk upstairs properly: the boy always put the same foot up ahead on each step - and she pointed this out to Luciano's mother, who had never realized. A different episode attesting to the teacher's sensible humanity occurred the next year when Luciano, thanks also to his mother's patient support and encouragement in the summer holidays, was doing better at school and had a brighter, broader outlook. It was at one of the "Fascist Saturday" meetings which the boys attended in their "Son of the She-Wolf" uniforms, standing in rows. Mrs. Ciabattoni was supposed to place in the front row the pupils who were dressed best, including the regulation black shoes. Luciano, like several others, only had brown shoes. In those days it was common for a boy not to own more than one pair; often cutting the toes off the old ones provided temporary relief before he was bought a new pair in the next size! So Mrs. Ciabattoni would gently explain to the pupils she could not put in the first row because of their shoes: "You are tall so stand behind the smaller boys, who would be out of sight otherwise!".
The first school year included weekly lessons in a music room, with a music teacher; there Luciano showed more promise. He learned that music is written on five horizontal lines, each note a symbol whose shape indicates the duration of the sound, while its upper or lower

position on the lines shows whether it is a high or low note. But the best part was singing, which the teacher, a charming lady Luciano was very fond of, taught and encouraged. She had a beautiful, carrying voice, whether speaking or singing, and her songs were lovely, easy melodies with simple words. Luciano learned fast and soon sang out enthusiastically as loudly as he could, hoping to attract the teacher's and others' attention. That vocal effort was perhaps a sort of revenge for the earlier unforgettable belly laughs!

No such simple wording applied to catechism, the summary of religious doctrine Luciano was supposed to become familiar with as preparation to receive the Christian sacrament of Communion, nor did those who briefed him use plain words. The boy was then in the second grade of primary school and could just about read. At the time the mass in Roman Catholic churches was still in Latin, which only a few people beside the clergy would understand. It was not until the Second Vatican Council of 1962, which opened under the pontificate of Pope John XXIII, that significant changes of the liturgy were authorized, including the use of modern languages in the celebrations, unleashing a wave of democratisation across the Catholic world. The mysteries of Latin could lead to some misinterpretation. Luciano's mother once told him about an amusing one. When she was sent to Alessandria as a teenager to learn embroidery from the French nuns, they also taught her the religious functions. Mom, for example, explained that *Domus Aurea* means "golden home" (standing for the house of God) and *Speculum Iustitiae* translates as "the mirror of justice". She told her son that the illiterate old women at the village in their litanies – the prayers by the officiant with alternate responses by the congregation – would turn these phrases round in the local dialect, according to how the Latin sounded to them; so the two above examples became: "Let's go to Alessandria" and "Big box of shoe polish"! But that was all so Luciano could get some fun out of religion, a subject soon to give him a few headaches. It wasn't just the prayers he had not bothered with before - the ones he repeated with his mother every night at bed-time were short and simple. Probably she had "tailored" them to help the boy grasp them better. When the war started she added one asking God to send our servicemen back home uninjured. Now it was no longer just sweet Mom who could help with divine matters which had only involved him marginally till then and left him unworried. Things were turning out challenging for several reasons, the main one being that he was being briefed as never before about obeying God's laws: God always knew everything about everybody; nothing could be hidden from him, not even one's thoughts. Possibly those who briefed him didn't insist enough on God's love for us, nor did they make sure the boy was not going to live his Christian credo as a threat. In any case he manfully tackled his religious training seriously, to begin with by paying unprecedented attention to "the rules of the game". He didn't simply learn the Ten Commandments and the prayers by heart - that was all he was expected to do; his introvert attitude prevailed and he tortured himself about what they meant, but he got nowhere and it only confused him. As to the Commandments, no wonder he could hardly cope with the sixth and the ninth; in the form he had been shown, they read more or less as: "You shall not commit impure acts" and "You shall not desire the woman who belongs to another". Prayers were also puzzling; what about: "..and blessed is the fruit of thy womb, Jesus..." as in the "Hail Mary"? Luciano's concept of birth was still based on what his mother had told him - she had found her first newborn under a sunflower! What's more, she had never updated him, nor had his notions got any clearer thanks to his limited contacts with other children of his own age, experience in a rural environment or elsewhere, though some help came from his older cousin Gabriele a couple of years later. Yet some of the boy's former beliefs were starting to wobble. One was about baby Jesus bringing him presents on Christmas night, as long as he had behaved himself. Up to then, behaving had been no problem; it was enough that he obeyed those who were entitled to obedience, currently his parents and virtually no-one else besides the teacher he adored. He was therefore fairly well adapted from the outset and had no recollections of anything like having temper tantrums.

After his father left for the war, no matter what his recommendations had been, the boy felt even more responsible and committed to Mom, proud and happy about it. But when he got involved with a good Christian's duties, as per the Commandments and the prayers that were new to him, his poor understanding proved a stumbling block. The prospect of obeying God seemed anything but straightforward and reassuring, what with the additional concern brought about by further briefings on confession, penance and sin? Eventually Luciano, turning back to his recent life with the fresh outlook provided by the catechism - never mind if it was flawed - figured out when and how he had failed to obey God's laws, and become a sinner.

At those times it was common, even for low middle-class families, to hire a maid, often a poor girl from the countryside, who would be pleased to have food and lodging and modest pay (there were no social security charges then!). Luciano's family was no exception and he heard a lot about Elsa, whom his parents had hired while in Asti and had kept up a lifetime friendship. He only remembered meeting her again much later after the war. His mother hired a maid in Belluno too, but she by no means resembled the quiet, nice, devoted Elsa and was soon dismissed. She never came back on time when she was sent out on an errand, apparently because she had many would-be boyfriends (Belluno hosted several barracks of the Alpine Corps and she was a pretty girl). Her stay with the family, even though short, nevertheless lasted long enough to arouse Luciano's interest, which she didn't discourage at all. It probably started with the boy having fun by playing innocent tricks like taking and hiding some of her household tools, for instance a broom. The boy's further jokes included acts no doubt stemming from his still pristine sexual instincts, partly reflecting increasing awareness of something peculiar and taboo happening in certain of his body parts you were not supposed to uncover. Very likely Luciano's maturing notions of sex, and growing curiosity about the opposite one, played an additional decisive role. He clearly recalls lying on the floor in a narrow passage, in the doorway between two rooms the maid would have to go through; he was only looking up at the ceiling until.....she came along, and both of them laughed (very few women wore trousers in those days, unless for horse-riding, skiing or the like). When the boy's mother saw one of these performances, of course she didn't laugh, but her reaction, most probably "soft" and not blaming the maid, if anything boosted her son's curiosity and interest in something which - hardly surprisingly - he felt was a strictly private matter to be shared only with the girl. Other memories of this maid, including further "private" games (when Luciano's mother was out with his three-years-younger sister), are much less detailed, except the time he stole some chocolate from the pantry, as a sympathy present to his "sweetheart" who was feeling homesick. There were definitely some physical contacts different from the previous episode, before Mom's complaint; presumably they were no more than very light "petting", with the girl most likely doing nothing more than stroking Luciano's head, or encouraging him – though it is unlikely – to take a more active, sexually-oriented role. He recalls no trace of any strong emotional involvement and this suggests he had filed away the overall "private" experience with the maid merely as a

49

curious, pointless but enjoyable game, with none of the lifelong negative mental "hangover" a child's premature, substantial sexual contact with an adult could entail. On the contrary it seems more likely that Luciano's childish "flirt" with the pretty girl was a healthy diversion from his frustrating, platonic enchantment with the "unattainable" schoolmate Marisa!

Luciano's guilty feeling for disobeying the sixth Commandment lingered, but, surprisingly enough in view of his past probity, he felt no such sentiment for either failing to listen to his mother's disapproval when playing with the maid, or stealing the chocolate. This might on the one hand have been due to the boy's confidence in his indulgent mother's proven disposition to mercy, but on the other he was concerned by the much less reassuring, elusive nature of the divine judgement he was meant to be subject to. In any case the power of the instinct (sexual!), no matter how infantile and primitive that drove Luciano's unprecedented behaviour, probably also dwarfed his apprehension about any later outcome, by making him feel he had acted naturally without any evil intent: there was nothing really worth worrying about much. In fact, he had no real trouble recognizing his presumed sin. The trouble occurred because of what followed in relation to confession (Luciano attended more briefings on admitting sin, on repentance and absolution). Most of all, however, another prayer set off the worst disturbing aspect in Luciano's whole initiation to religion. Unlike the amusing litanies of the old illiterate women of the village, as recounted by his mother, no Latin was involved, but what seemed to the boy the clumsy wording of the prayer named "*Act of Contrition*" played a mean trick on him, who had learned it by heart repeating each sentence as he had heard it. While the prayer actually read something like: "I promise to escape any occasion for sin", he had mistakenly memorized it as:" I promise to escape on occasion" and repeated that promise at least once a day as recommended! Luciano had indeed heard obscure, scary tales of boys who had left their homes, and always thought that was nonsense. Luciano had indeed heard obscure, scary tales of boys who had left their homes, and always thought that was nonsense. However, unaware of having misunderstood the prayer, by saying it that odd way, he was promising to do something he would have never dared do. Thus Luciano faced a conundrum: because of his failure to maintain the promise, as penance for a sin, he would not receive absolution. Luckily enough this kind of distressing deadlock didn't last too long:

eventually the time for confession came.

Rather than kneeling in one of those frightening boxes in a dark corner of the church, hiding the confessor, the boy fortunately met a nice, smart clergyman in his office who noticed at once that he was scared and swiftly dealt with that, promptly earning the little sinner's confidence. Luciano could at last open his heart and was relieved of the burden he had carried for so long all alone! The affable man listened, nodding in encouragement, and didn't say much; he merely reassured the boy, who badly needed it, and shortly after that came the day when he received the sacrament of Communion, unworried. Such a day, he was told, several great figures of history regarded as the best in their lives: did he feel the same way? Possibly, but only because he had just been released from the nightmare of his challenging first religious experience.

Giacomo Leopardi, one of the great poets of the 19th century, whose art was most influenced by the contemporary "philosopher of pessimism" Arthur Schopenhauer, in his touching poem describing the clearing of the air after the storm as a metaphor of the human condition, wrote that pleasure is "the son of sorrow" and joy nothing more but relief from previous fear.

Asti, 1937: Luciano as portrayed by his Dad

Asti, 1937: a convalescent Luciano being cheered up by his Dad wearing a Borsalino hat

Cervo Ligure, 1937: Luciano, with aunt Tina (left) and Mom, first sees the sea-side

Palombina, 1938: behind that row of thick shrubs sat Luciano's beloved wrecked cars

Ancona, 1939: Luciano struggles to learn the military commmands

Pietra Marazzi,1941:
Luciano hails Dad's
new car, a FIAT
500A

Belluno, 1941: Luciano with Mom and little sister
Gabriella on the banks of the River Piave

Belluno, 1941: did that radio play Lili Marlene?

Belluno, 1942: were those the stamps Luciano dropped on Marlisa's terrace?

Venice, 1942: Luciano with Mom and little sister Gabriella

San Vito, 1942: Dad took us quite close to Mount Antelao

Borca, 1942: Luciano and Mount Pelmo way behind

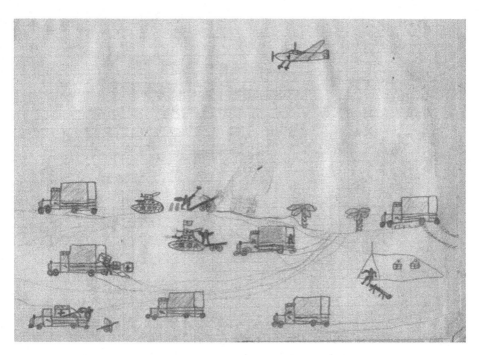

Warfare scenes as seen by Luciano aged eight

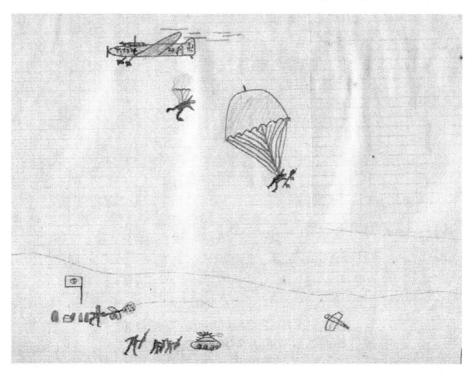

*Belluno: the Aristide Gabelli public
primary school in the Nineteen thirties*

*Belluno,1942: The Opera Nazionale
Balilla building in Segato Street*

7. The End of an Era

Fascism revived the pomp of the ancient Roman Empire, adopting many of its symbols. To begin with it named itself after the *fasces* (a bundle of wooden rods wound round an axe, borne before Roman magistrates as a badge of authority). Thus, Mussolini decided a new Fascist era had started with his advent to power (the "March on Rome" of 28 October 1922) and that from then on the years should be displayed in Roman numerals, like in the Julian calendar, *ab urbe condita* (AUC), meaning, in Latin, from the founding of the city [of Rome in the year 753 BC].

In 1943, year XXI of the Fascist era, Luciano, almost eight years old, was about to complete the second grade of primary school in Belluno. He couldn't know he was destined to spend only a few more months there, up to the summer vacations. Then, on July 25, with Mussolini's overthrow the Fascist era suddenly ended.

What had looked like a purely European war at the outset, when in June 1940 the Italian *Duce* decided to take Hitler's side against England and France, turned into the worst-ever world conflict with the German invasion of Russia on 22 June 1941. The American Congress declared war on Japan on 8 December that year, 24 hours after its unannounced strike against the U.S. naval base at Pearl Harbor. Italy, ill prepared and even less adequately equipped, followed its June 1940 incursion through the Alps into France - already surrendering to the German armies - with a succession of military disasters. First came the invasion of Greece in October; Mussolini wanted to impress Hitler, but the Germans were obliged to rescue the Italian forces early in 1941. The Germans also backed Italy in the hard-fought campaigns of North Africa. After a first Italian move from Cyrenaica (present-day Libya) into British-held Egypt in September 1940, the British struck back early in December relying on many more tanks, performing much better than the obsolete Italian ones; by January 1941, they had conquered most of Cyrenaica and taken over 100,000 prisoners. But in February Hitler sent a young general, Erwin Rommel, with two mechanized divisions. He led the joint German and Italian forces and was rapidly and brilliantly successful. The British retreated precipitously into Egypt, losing many of their tanks and leaving a wealth of supplies, a blessing for the exhausted Italians. By mid-April most of Cyrenaica had been re-conquered. This triumph was heralded proudly in Fascist Italy and the opinion spread that, with German help, the outcome of the North African conflict could turn favorable. Luciano meanwhile was learning about some of the epics from the war song "*Giarabub*" (a Libyan oasis on the Egyptian border) celebrating the heroic conduct of the Italians there: "Colonel, I want no bread; for my musket give me lead!".

Rommel, known as the Desert Fox because of his skilful leadership, is regarded as one of the best, as well as humane, commanders in World War II. Following his involvement in the failed conspiracy to overthrow Hitler of 20 July 1944, Rommel was secretly obliged to commit suicide, although he was publicly mourned as a national hero. Regardless of the general's further successes up till mid-1942, and several further episodes of heroic conduct, like those of the Italian paratroopers of the *Folgore* division in the October battles at el-Alamein - admired even by enemies - the Axis forces were eventually overwhelmed by the Allies' superiority. (Axis was the name taken by the three powers Germany, Italy and Japan when they signed the tripartite pact against the Allied nations on 27 September 1940 in Berlin; Hungary, Romania, Slovakia and Bulgaria joined later). This was also thanks to the U.S. troops landing on the western coast of North Africa in November. By May 1943 North Africa was completely in Allied hands. Before then, though, in 1941, Italy had lost its eastern African colonies including Eritrea, Ethiopia and Somalia.

The Italian Army sent to Russia in July 1941 to support to the Germans (known as ARMIR , about 250,000 troops) suffered untold hardship. Fewer than 150,000 made it home in January 1943; more than 30,000 were wounded and 54,000 had died in captivity. On 10 July 1943 Allied seaborne troops landed in Sicily. This invasion of the island meant an immediate threat to the Italian mainland. A few days later, on the 19th, at a meeting with Hitler who had asked to see him urgently, Mussolini pleaded for help, specifically weapons (planes) which the *Fuhrer* refused. Those Germany had sent before had mostly been destroyed on the ground by the enemy because they had not been properly hidden. Moreover, he had just learned the Russians were threatening an offensive on the eastern front.

Curiously, the two met (discreetly) in Feltre, a small town close to Belluno where Luciano lived at that time. Mario, the boy's father, notified by a Roman friend who was a member of the Duce's staff, rushed there with his Leica (model 3b 1939, the "mythical" German camera still used up till the mid-20th century by such noted photographers as Henri Cartier-Bresson and Robert Capa), wearing the uniform of the paramilitary National Security Volunteer Militia. Luciano was quite excited to know his father was going to be so close to Mussolini, but disappointed when he learned he had had to hand over the exposed films to that friend of his! Yet many years later when grey-haired, sorting through his late father's archives Luciano stumbled across a curious photograph of the two tragic leaders – Mussolini surprisingly wearing sunglasses – with the date and place (*Villa Gaggia*) of their meeting handwritten on the back. Had Mario smuggled out any of his films (unlikely) or had he been sent that photo by his friend attending the Duce?

The very day Hitler and Mussolini were meeting in Feltre, the Allies' planes dropped bombs on Rome. Other Italian towns had been bombed before, but nobody expected it to happen to the capital. The astounding news spread despair throughout the already disheartened country: was it the last drop that makes the cup run over? A series of painful defeats had eroded confidence in the Duce, not only of a large part of the population but also of many Italian Fascist leaders. On the night of 24-25 July 1943, the majority of the Fascist Grand Council voted a resolution against Mussolini; he resigned and the next morning king Victor Emmanuel III ordered his arrest and entrusted Marshal Pietro Badoglio, the Royal Army Chief of Staff, with forming a new government.

Could Luciano, a boy of about eight living in an apparently still quiet, out-of-the-way township like Belluno, ever grasp the far-off developments and the atrocity of the war, or even the domestic turnabout in summer 1943? Never mind, they still affected him. Earlier in July his father's cousin Luigi Amelotti, then about 20, a private in the army, had visited Belluno on a short leave from the Greek front and brought a most welcome bottle of olive oil. To his parent's consternation, nobody heard of him afterwards, until he showed up as a "miracle" from a German concentration camp, when the war ended.

A bigger "miracle" blessing Luciano was his father surviving the Italian Army's ruinous retreat from Russia. Why had Mario Manara voluntarily joined the eastern front? The boy learned the reason from him quite a few years later: it was a matter of both conscience and career. Conscience-wise Mario felt a bit of a guilty stay-at-home while so many Italian youths were risking their lives on the battlefields. For years Mario had inspired boys to feel patriotic and most likely many of them, now grown up, were servicemen at war where he too should have been sharing their fate. Career-wise, Luciano's father in the past few years had suffered some drawbacks and not taking part in the war would only have made them worse.

From the outset he had worked as a local manager with the national foundation for youth welfare and patriotic education (*Opera Nazionale Balilla* – ONB). Although established in 1926 with an *ad hoc* law Mussolini had specifically wanted, the ONB was not part of the Fascist Party. Under the authority of the Ministry of Education its task was to promote physical education in the schools and sport and summer camps at the seaside and in the mountains; these were genuinely popular, though not obligatory. It also ran vocational and rural schools.

Renato Ricci, with two bronze medals as a former shock troops volunteer in World War I when less than 20, and bold leader of Fascist squads in Tuscany after the war, was appointed boss of the foundation as Secretary of Education. In shaping ONB he looked for advice abroad too, approaching Baden-Powell, the founder of the Scout Movement, and some promoters of the German Bauhaus school of design. Mario Manara became one of Mr. Ricci's most dedicated young henchmen. One of his major achievements was organizing and leading a cruise for ONB youth to South America in 1936, on board the luxury ocean liner *Count Biancamano*. The unusual passengers were an elite section - the *Marinaretti* (little mariners) - of the 14-18 year-old boys (*Balillas*) who wore uniforms like the Italian Royal Navy; possibly a good deal of them came from upper-class homes. In spite of the almost military discipline imposed on the obviously high-spirited boys and several mentors looking after their crew of around 70 day and night, Mario had little time to relax throughout the journey; however, everything went well, the youths were greeted most cordially everywhere, especially by the Italians living in the different places visited. Mario's endeavour was rewarded by the boys' enthusiasm and praise from his boss. Thanks to that opportunity Luciano's Dad could briefly embrace his father in Buenos Aires, whom he had last seen at home as a teenager.

When Luciano was born, Mario – still a young 28 - had already been appointed President of the ONB section in Asti, the head town of one of Piedmont's provinces. The ONB proved one of the most successful and popular of Mussolini's undertakings but had powerful opponents in the Fascist Party, who prevailed in 1937. The Duce put an end to the ONB which was stripped of its activities, taken over by the party and renamed *Gioventù Italiana del Littorio* (GIL, Italian youth of the Lictor) from the ancient Roman Lictors who carried the fasces while attending the magistrates. That was a real blow for Luciano's father who ended up unhappily in the GIL section of the small, oddly located Belluno. There he very much missed his former boss: when Mussolini sent Renato Ricci, like all the other ministers, to Greece for the war, Mario asked to join him but he refused: "Stay home, you've got a wife and children!".

Eventually Mario found his way to go to war. Having been discharged from the Royal Army reserve because no longer physically fit, as a keen amateur photographer he managed to be appointed war correspondent by the LUCE film institute and in the summer of 1942 volunteered for the Russian front with the rank of "centurion" (meaning captain - one more example of Fascism's revival of imperial Rome's pomp) in the Militia, the Fascist paramilitary corps. The LUCE had been established by Mussolini in 1925 as a non-profit organization aimed at using the cinema to foster education and national values. Its main output was newsreels, i.e. short filmed news stories regularly released in movie theatres before the main show (as was customary world-wide until the 1960s when television news broadcasts completely superseded them). The LUCE in the third millennium is still a valuable archive of (digital) photographic and filmed records and a producer of historical documentaries and home videos based on them.

Luciano hardly noticed the turnabout that started with Mussolini's overthrow. Jubilant demonstrations were limited; there were none in Belluno, although the most obvious signs of the Fascist regime were torn down. The war continued, but Pietro Badoglio, the new head of the government, was secretly negotiating with the Allies a volte-face which would have proved a tragedy, since there were still considerable German forces in Italy. However, the boy learned something strange about Badoglio, since his mother happened to have met him a few years earlier, close to Luciano's birthplace Asti. Pietro Badoglio, an army officer with an increasingly prominent but controversial and equivocal role in Italy throughout the first half of the 20th century, was appointed general in World War I, regardless of his involvement in the Caporetto rout. With the advent of Fascism, he rose to the top in the Italian Army in spite of his tepid relationship with

Mussolini. King Victor Emmanuel III appointed him Duke of Addis Ababa after the conquest of Ethiopia in May 1936, which he described in detail in a book, "*The war of Ethiopia*", richly illustrated with maps and photos. It was in September of that year that Luciano's parents were invited for a celebration in a villa donated to the Duke by his fellow citizens of Grazzano Monferrato in Asti province (from then on renamed Grazzano Badoglio). The general concluded from their close resemblance that they must have been brother and sister! Reportedly Badoglio was used to making such tactless comments, even in public!

Luciano of course hardly noticed the wartime events while he was living in Belluno, nor did he feel their unwanted impact on his family's life, with the major exception of his father's long absence. Fortunately he was never troubled by doubts that Dad might not make it back home, and in fact eagerly looked forward to his return. How could Luciano ever forget the day when his teacher called him out of the classroom and he only just managed to recognize his pallid veteran father wearing a uniform which looked far too big, but ran straight into his open arms! Shortly before leaving Belluno for Russia in 1942, Mario had arranged to spend a weekend with his family in nearby Venice. That trip too proved unforgettable. Luciano was not old enough to fully appreciate that jewel of a city, acknowledged as part of the artistic and architectural patrimony of all humanity. No doubt, however, like any new visitor, he must have felt transported into a different world whose atmosphere and beauty remain incomparable. He left there with unforgettable childish recollections, either amusing, like "streets flooded with water so that boats could go by", or scary, like the "Piombi" prison, or in-between (the "towering" boatman who stood on the unbelievably high stern of the pitch-black gondola and looked down on him while punting: was he Charon, the mythical ferryman who carries the souls of the dead across the rivers in the underworld ?

While in Belluno, besides Venice Luciano visited some other nearby sites of interest. One worth mentioning, 25 miles to the north, is Cortina in the midst of some of the most spectacular peaks of the Dolomite Alps. Already a renowned ski resort, it was originally selected as the site for the 1944 Olympic winter games which were cancelled because of World War II. There the boy spent part of his summer vacations of 1942 and 1943; actually he stayed a few miles south of Cortina, with his mother and younger sister, in a former luxury hotel that had been destined to be converted to host Fascist youth summer camps. It lay midway between the villages of San Vito

- further north - and Borca down toward the south. Nobody lived there but the janitor, his wife and a goat whose bitter-tasting milk Luciano disliked. The spectacular four-storey stone building seemed really big, surrounded by a huge pine wood, copiously dotted with cyclamens and tiny but heavenly scented wild strawberries. On the east the park was bordered by the national highway and the parallel narrow-gauge railway, both climbing to Cortina. These had been cut out, like the broad terrace on which the hotel stood, on the steep scree slope where one could still see remains of World War I battles. It was overlooked by a towering, overhanging cliff, Mount Antelao. On the opposite side – to the west - the pine tree-lined slope dropped steeply for several hundred yards down to the crystal-clear stream Boite, home of mountain trout, flowing southward in the narrow valley named after it. Further to the west the hotel looked out onto another fir tree-lined slope gently rising from the opposite flank of the Boite Valley, and the more distant armchair-shaped Mount Pelmo. Luciano never returned there, but his recollections are remarkably vivid of that masterly pictorial landscape composed only of green woodlands, and majestic cliffs shining under clear skies: that must have been the first time the boy was struck by the imposing beauty of untainted nature. One rainy day Luciano begged Basilio, the janitor, to tour the building with him. The grand ballroom on the first floor opened onto a grandiose stairway facing the fountain in the middle of a garden surrounded by the park; photos still hanging on the walls showed elegant guests, mostly celebrities Basilio was proudly listing. Led by an unusual, enticing scent, the boy and his escort entered a dimly lit room and found a safe; it wasn't locked and once fully opened it proved empty. Yet the boy felt that scent was stronger and didn't give up: he moved closer and boldly probed its depths, stretching his arm inside. Triumphantly Luciano drew back the arm holding tight onto a "treasure": a bar of fine toilet soap! Three years after the war started, such luxurious items were hardly available any longer and Luciano washed – reluctantly, when his mother insisted - with the same nasty smelly bar used for laundry!

A few days before Luciano was meant to leave Belluno for good and resettle in Piedmont in his ancestors' home, two undesirable-looking visitors knocked at the apartment door, just while Mom and aunt Cristina were busy packing everything. The men were police officers charged with searching the residences of former executives of the Fascist party (including Luciano's father, who was away).They wore civilian clothes and acted courteously, but nonetheless their job took at least a couple of days, and to the boy's mother's and aunt's dismay involved undoing all the packages ready for shipment. Luciano curiously was not at all upset by their arrival and "sided" with the newcomers; he offered his help, asked whether there was anything special they were looking for that he might find, and brought them a box containing some of his toys which he proudly showed them. After all those boring days which kept him at home while his mother and aunt were packing, the boy had finally met someone to play with! Apparently the intruders did not dislike that surprisingly chatty boy and couldn't help letting him "collaborate" all the time! They didn't find anything of interest except an old pistol (it had belonged to Luciano's grandfather Carlo) which they took away. Luciano's father (who knew those men) was very upset on learning of their visit; he met them not long after (a couple of months later) and it was not to say thank you! When he returned to Belluno to ship everything, the turnaround of July 25 had been reversed following Mussolini's rescue by the Germans on September 12 and his establishment of a new Fascist state in Northern Italy.

While Mother and aunt Tina were packing, Luciano too was getting ready to leave in his own small way. In his "virtual" suitcase he had unconsciously packed lasting memories, the many good impressions of his stay in that lovely little town, so friendly that in winter he could play safely in the streets with his baby sleigh!. In that "multimedia" bag he fitted a wide range of items, from the anthems he had learned by heart as played by the bands of the Alpine Corps whose barracks were in Belluno, to the hours spent with carpenters; typographers, and machinists in the workshops at the GIL-sponsored vocational schools. There the boy glowed with excitement and admiration, which earned him the men's constant patient attention. It must have been there that he first developed his lifelong feeling of sincere respect for craftsmanship and for those engaged in it with pride, and the conviction that their greatest reward was the awareness of having done a good job. Alongside his life-long fancy for cars, Luciano, as an adult loved tinkering with their engines, like Larry, the main character in the novel "*The razor's edge*", by the well-known 20th- century British author Somerset Maugham. Luciano too, whenever he felt bogged down with study, took time off for a spell of manual labor which always proved "spiritually invigorating".

8. Back Where He Belonged

When they left Belluno in summer 1943 Luciano's parents had planned to resettle in an apartment in the building belonging to Joe, the boy's maternal grandfather, in Alessandria. They moved most of their belongings there but, fearing air raids by the Allies, decided it was safer to live in the nearby countryside – never mind that at that time most of the comforts of urban housing were lacking, running water to begin with. They stayed in Pietra Marazzi (known largely simply as *Pietra*, meaning stone in Italian) and got organized in a part of Luciano's grandmother Giuseppina's house she had previously let out. Electricity was available only for lighting and small appliances such as a radio receiver, but not for heating or cooking, which were both provided by a fireplace and a stove on the ground floor; their chimneys passed through the two bedrooms upstairs, giving off some slight heat, but the only other source of heating was pans which fitted under raised frames that were placed under the blankets some time before going to bed.

Since ice, which in winter formed strange, beautiful crystals on the inside of the bedroom window panes, was not available at the village, a basket was lowered on a rope into the fairly deep well, and this served as the icebox. Luciano's father had a petrol barrel cut by a blacksmith, who also made a stand for it - that was the bathtub! These shortcomings hardly bothered Luciano, but other aspects of that rather rough rural living amused him. One was the huge variety of fowls freely scratching about all around the house, except in the "front" garden and the vegetable garden which had been fenced. To add to grandmother Giuseppina's few hens and cockerels the boy had already met, his mother bought more chicks, including ducks and turkeys. The "animal farm" also boasted two pigs. Raising them and the chicks was quite a job for Giuseppina and Luciano's mother, but they turned out to be a blessing to feed the family in those years of hand-to-mouth existence. Giuseppina, who farmed her own cultivable land, was fortunate in that she was entitled to keep some flour from the wheat harvest (otherwise it was obligatorily sold to the public authority-controlled stores). She could also have goods baked at the village bakery. Luciano in fact – though he was not aware of it - fared enviably better than those who could not leave the towns (which were soon exposed to air raids) and find shelter elsewhere, like his family.

Although the war had spread on the Italian soil in summer 1943 with the surprising invasion of Sicily by the Allies, their advance through the south of mainland Italy was quite slow. It was firmly checked by the Germans and their loyal Italian forces; the Allies entered Rome only in June of the following year and in the north of the country actual combat was still felt as a distant threat.

Luciano, while enjoying that last period of relative tranquillity, developed in several important directions, contributing further to the growth of his personality. The main one was schooling. The boy enrolled in the third grade and within a few months he turned out to be a good student and acquired unprecedented self-confidence. That great leap, surprising in view of his difficulties when he had started school in Belluno two years earlier, stemmed from several favorable events: one was that he started to read eagerly when he met a young doctor.

Carlo Roggero was an obstetrician working at the Alessandria hospital who, because of the war, had temporarily left his home there to settle in Pietra with his family, in the house next door across the shrub hedge, belonging to Giuseppina's sister Francesca. Carlo already had a four-year-old daughter and the couple had another child two years later, but as Luciano approached him, fascinated by his motorcycle, he developed a deep affection for the boy which lasted throughout his life. It was Carlo who introduced Luciano to a "Boys' Encyclopedia" and lent it to him, one volume at a time. That proved a mine of excitement where he could nourish his innate curiosity and learn about people, places and, best of all, how things are made and work. Carlo would also welcome his little friend's inquiries and answered thoughtfully. This fostered the boy's inquisitive nature, which eventually materialized into his lifelong professional interest in science.

Another incentive came from aunt Tina, the kindergarten teacher; she too encouraged Luciano to read, but differently, offering him fiction by two authors of the second half of the 19th century; she and her brother, the boy's father, had saved the books from their youth. First came some of the works by an Italian author of action and adventure, Emilio Salgari. After failing to become a naval officer – in line with his juvenile passion to explore the seas - he turned to writing tales set in exotic locations, although he probably never crossed the frontiers of Italy. His heroes were mostly pirates and outlaws Sandokan is the best known – and fights against greed, tyranny and corruption. Salgari's numerous novels have been read by generations of youngsters for over a century and adapted as comics, animated series and feature films. Though little known in the English-speaking world, he has been popular in Europe as well as in Latin America where he is considered a forerunner of anti-imperialistic writing. Salgari's captivating pages magically transported Luciano into a fantastic world: he cruised aboard Sandokan's vessels to live the boldest undertakings and combat injustice at his side. A feeling of romance too enchanted the boy when, in "*The Tigers of Mompracem*", the pirate, Sandokan, a former Bornean prince, learns of a beautiful girl known as the Pearl of Labuan, and that changes his life. The author's dealing with Sandokan's love affair in strictly platonic terms swayed Luciano and strengthened his tendency to idealize. Thus whereas Salgari's readings were an incitement to boldness against injustice and evil, they didn't help much when he took a fancy to a girl at school: he viewed her as a sort of stunning deity and once again, like when he met Marisa in first grade, he hardly dared even look at Ilia!

A quite different book, also given to Luciano by aunt Tina, was "*Cuore*" (Heart) by Edmondo De Amicis, who embraced journalism as well as novels and travel writing after renouncing a successful military career in the army of the new Kingdom of Italy; apparently he had been put off by the cruel spectacle left after the defeat of the Italian forces in the battle of Custoza (1866) where he had fought against the Austrians. *Cuore* is a children's novel in diary form as fictionally written by a eight-year old boy from a wealthy, educated household, in the third grade at a primary school where his classmates are mostly from working class families. The boy writer records his interactions with school fellows and the teacher; his homework includes reading tales (shown in the book) about exemplary children, that exalt moral values and love of the home country.

Cuore's success was spectacular. In only a few months dozens of Italian editions were sold out. Translations into various languages, including Chinese, followed; the Spanish version, *Corazón* meaning "Heart", was very popular in Latin America right up into the 1970s. This book too was little known in the English-speaking countries, but was reportedly widely read and valued among Israel's youth in the

1950s. Movies and animated series from *Cuore* were released in different languages all over the world.

Fascist Italy mainly welcomed *Cuore* because it fostered patriotism, but after World War II it fell into neglect as rhetorical and old-fashioned and was soon virtually unknown to subsequent generations of young Italians. No doubt reading Salgari and De Amicis influenced Luciano's developing ethics and impressed him with virtuous examples, exalting qualities like loyalty, gratitude, respect, generosity, sympathy for the poor and so forth. Thinking back as an adult to this sort of "imprinting", he found himself wondering whether some of his later achievements had in fact been deeply rooted in it or were just due to good luck. Yet at times he blamed a not altogether extinguished romantic, idealistic boyhood heritage for some of his major failures! Never, later in life, did Luciano find a fictional character as inspiring as those in these pristine books, with the sole possible exception of Arrowsmith, the "child" of the first American Nobel Laureate for literature, Sinclair Lewis, in his Pulitzer Prize-winning novel.

Luciano's juvenile readings also included translations of foreign classics like "*Twenty Thousand Leagues Under the Sea*" by the French author Jules Verne, "*Robinson Crusoe*" by the British writer Daniel Defoe, and "*The Paul Street Boys*" by the Hungarian Ferenc Molnár. Some he had received from his father, others he found in the parish library where he met Don Cesare, a priest he was to appreciate greatly in the years to follow.

What else, besides some helpful readings, pushed Luciano to do well at school and feel at ease there? Self-confidence in dealing with the teacher, Miss Pia Baldi (who happened to be a dear friend of aunt Tina's and liked him at first sight – and he noticed it!) and classmates, no doubt mattered. Most of his classmates, boys and girls, were from local households where, with few exceptions, dialect was the preferred language at the time; no wonder they felt uneasy with proper Italian - and often asked Luciano for help. The other pupils had moved temporarily to the village from nearby Alessandria because of the war, but neither they nor the locals had seen much of "the rest of the world" (including the sea) like Luciano who, besides having lived in different parts of his home country, was more used to speaking and listening to adults than to children of his own age. His above-average knowledge meant that his conversation was fluent and he wrote well, despite his bad handwriting! Math, though, he struggled with. Despite these apparent advantages, however, Luciano, though proficient in Italian, never came first in his class. He disliked the idea, as well as several of the topics he was expected to study – first of all those requiring rote learning ("learning by heart").

His newly gained self-reliance favored his integration; he liked all his new schoolmates and they liked him: school was fun except that ... Luciano was bewitched by the beautiful Ilia Boffi and didn't know how to cope with his feelings. With everybody else at school save Ilia, Luciano was by no means shy. He still has recollections of only a few other girls in his class. Like them, Ilia was agreeable, kind and simple-mannered; all the girls wore an almost heel-length school smock. It must have been her face, appearance, smile, and grace of bearing that made the difference and caught Luciano's eye. The celebrated French filmmaker Francois Truffaut's *"L'argent de Poche"* (Pocket money, 1976), describes a year of school life of young children in a small town in central France and masterly portrays the touching first kiss of Patrick and Martine. Luciano could have hardly imagined doing anything so brave with Ilia; just holding "his" sweetheart's hand would already have seemed daring!

Was a timid, practically "virtual" kind of kiss an impure act, a sort of sin? Quite possibly. Some sexophobic influence was inherent in the catechism the boy had learned in Belluno in preparation for his first Christian Communion. As to kissing, shortly before school started in Pietra Marazzi, Luciano had received an "unforeseen, silent, warning message" from his father, because of a flip book. A flip book was a booklet whose pages, showing a series of drawings that vary only slightly from one page to the next, are stapled at the bottom, to be held with one hand, while the thumb of the other hand flips through the pages at the top; the rapidly turning pages give the illusion of objects in motion and provide a primitive form of movies. Luciano had read about the 19th-century invention of that gadget in Carlo Roggero's Boys' Encyclopedia and, shortly afterwards, by chance, received a contemporary war propaganda version (most probably from cousin Gabriele). A bold Italian serviceman runs, heedless of fire, into an enemy trench to kick out a scared Briton (recognizable from his wide-brimmed helmet of those times); then he turns and runs back, ending up in the open arms of a pretty girl waiting at home: they kiss passionately. The boy couldn't wait to share that new "technological" toy with his father, but when he did the reaction was unexpected; after the less than 15-second-long show was over, Dad frowned at Luciano and said nothing. The boy's embarrassment was short-lived: he walked away in search of a tool

and tore up the flip book's last few pages where the pretty girl appeared. Then Luciano showed the edited "movie" to his surprised, speechless parent who smiled brightly while embracing him tight!
Luciano's crush on Ilia remained steadfast for quite a long time, even though the following school year they were no longer classmates. After the war, when both lived in Alessandria, they met by chance only occasionally and just said "hello" to each other. The boy never told anybody about that object of deep affection that he saved jealously as his dearest open-eyes dream. Only later on, as a teenager, Luciano was less troubled by a romantic, more sexually oriented interest in other girls at school, and Ilia's memory faded, though never completely, nor did he ever feel such a pure, heavenly sentiment again.

Once school was completed, there was no reason to worry that Luciano might give up his favorite amusements and waste the rest of the day regretting his lack of action toward that admired classmate. His preferred games while growing up in Pietra tended to involve a search for novelty and in fact he turned to "inventing" most of his new toys. He found some helpful hints in the Boys' Encyclopedia his friend the doctor was lending him. There he first learned about fireworks which he found "fatally" attractive: gunpowder was their secret. This is why, when he read about the black powder, which consisted of a mix of sulphur, charcoal, and potassium nitrate, he set out to search for these ingredients. Charcoal abounded among the ashes of the spent fire, potassium nitrate was nothing but saltpetre, the white stuff he could scrape off the old buildings' exposed brick walls, which were encrusted with it. As to sulphur, Luciano knew grandfather Joe used it in the vineyard, to protect grapes from their specific pest, but...... how to get hold of it? This was worth discussing with his cousin Gabriele.
Gabriele, the son of Gemma, Luciano's Mom's elder sister, though
only two or three years older than Luciano, could teach him a lot - good and bad. It was Gabriele, not long before, who had briefed his junior cousin about how babies were born from their mother's womb; there was no mention of the father's role. Thus Luciano, while gaining a substantial – though only partial – picture of the issue (until then he had trusted his parents' "politically correct" version that they had found him under a sunflower), still had a lot more to discover about human reproductive physiology.
Gabriele ruled out upsetting Joe by asking him for something he had plenty of good reasons to keep out of the reach of children, but promised to look around to see whether sulphur was easier to get

elsewhere. Luciano had almost forgotten the hunt for sulphur when, quite a bit later, Gabriele showed up with an unforeseen solution: he brought some gunpowder (smokeless) of the kind used in ammunition for contemporary firearms - it seems he had taken apart a shotgun cartridge lost by a hunter. However, after the chaos of the days following the armistice of 8 September 1943, including the evasions from barracks, all sort of military weaponry had been stolen and some ended up in the hands of boys of Gabriele's age. Luciano himself was similarly involved a year later. Getting the explosive stuff from his cousin was not cheap; probably the deal involved trading quite a few metal and colored glass marbles, or something else he was loath to give away. Oddly, Gabriele, only after tucking the marbles or whatever Luciano had given him as the reward away in his pockets, cautioned about the inherent dangers of that kind of gunpowder, which one should never ignite directly with a match, but a fuse should be set. Luciano knew that a fuse consisted of some sort of flammable cord that enabled you to set off an explosive with some delay from a distance.

Better late than never, but our little hero not only started to doubt whether he was on the right track trying to fabricate fireworks - the project actually looked like being troublesome. He didn't ask Gabriele's help to obtain a fuse and fretted only about how to choose the right place to hide the tiny jar containing a few pinches of gunpowder.

When eventually Luciano made up his mind - the idea that he should try something prevailed over his anxiety, though it didn't go away – and "dug up" his mini-arsenal, he had figured out what to do. It was a lovely late summer evening after dinner; the boy's parents, grandmother Giuseppina and aunt Tina were chatting in the garden as usual; his little sister too was there. Luciano sneaked into the kitchen where the smoldering fire, where his mother had only warmed some water for washing the dishes, was designated as the "firing range". He had already spent the previous days reasoning that no matter how pitiful the explosive might turn out to be, testing only a few grains didn't seem like folly, so he carried on. With his right arm stretched out and no more than ten minute thin flat scales of gunpowder firmly held between thumb and forefinger, Luciano approached the fireplace (almost boldly) just near enough to be able to drop them one by one onto the ashes where some embers still glowed. To his delight (and reassurance), this cautious move produced a few pleasing, bright, colorful puffs you might think were

Lilliputian fireworks. He continued with his new game for a while and got better results as he dropped a little more gunpowder each time. However, he soon got bored with that and did...the wrong thing! He poured most of the powder left in the little jar onto a piece of paper the size of a playing card which he then wrapped up like a candy. After throwing that wicked bundle into the fireplace, Luciano ran away to the far side of the kitchen, but nothing happened for several minutes. The situation was embarrassing and he felt he should not leave things like that and say nothing to his parents, but how would he face them?

Sunset advanced and he had not much time left before the party outside in the garden would break up and they would all come back indoors. Luciano thought he should try to revive the fire and moved in to do so in the worst possible way; he intended to blow onto the ashes by getting close to them with his head leaning into the fireplace! But he had not even started puffing when...... WHOOOOM !! An enormous rumbling flash filled the fireplace and completely dazzled the boy, who fell dumb to the floor, scared to death, with his face burning. There was a bad smell like burnt feathers (Luciano had smelled these when grandmother had set fire to a dirty old cushion). But it took him less than a couple of minutes to realize he was by no means badly injured. Thus, especially since he could see no damage in the room, his only concern became what he would look like to his parents and relatives outside, as they were likely to question him.

Luciano rushed upstairs and washed his face. In the mirror it looked just a bit reddish, but ...where had his eyebrows gone? - and there were patches of missing hair! Would they grow back? In any case what mattered at the moment was only to cover up his messy appearance as well as possible (besides "obscuring" the smell of burnt feathers). Some perfumed brilliantine (a cream for making hair glossy) belonging to his father deceivingly seemed the ideal remedy; it was actually more likely to make things worse by calling attention to the "culprit" from a distance! After a short while Luciano sauntered out and showed himself to the unaware household. At that point the shock of the frightening explosion - which he had repressed too soon while overrating the feared consequences of his misdeed- unexpectedly emerged. He could not help bursting into tears; visibly shocked, and without being asked, he somehow confusedly described what he had done to the adults. They didn't even think of reproaching him, but, relieved by the fact that he had not suffered any serious consequences, made efforts to comfort him. It was his father who hugged him first – even though not long before he had left some red signs on Luciano's lower legs by punishingly "massaging" them with a tiny willow shoot: without telling his parents, Luciano had not come straight home from school and only hours later he'd been found at a classmate's place.

Luciano escaped harm not only with the gunpowder, but several other times during the war, when he got more seriously involved with firearms and ammunition. Although he and his peers who couldn't resist playing these risky games were surprisingly knowledgeable on the matter, good luck mostly accounted for those who were never injured. However, whether because of risky games or other causes, after the war, besides the many who died, it was tragically common to meet disabled boys; some had lost their parents too.

Carlo Gnocchi was a former military chaplain who had served in Italy's Alpine regiment in the Russian campaign and assisted soldiers and war orphans. After the war, he devoted his life to the needy and eventually decided to dedicate himself entirely to works of charity. Thus, while Milan was being rebuilt, Don Gnocchi worked to "rebuild the human person", gathering orphans and children, victims of war, and offering them help and education. That started from scratch as the *Città dei Ragazzi* (the boys' town) to become a foundation providing medical care for thousands of patients in over 70 hospitals in Europe; the Foundation does scientific research too. In October 2009 Milan hosted Don Gnocchi's ceremony of beatification by the Catholic Church.

9. Down by the Riverside

The Marengo plain stretches northward across the River Bormida up to the River Tanaro; the two merge less than two miles north-east of Alessandria, just before passing the village of Pietra Marazzi on the left bank. The confluence, which witnessed Napoleon's epochal victory over the Austrians in June 1800, is mentioned by renowned Italian writers of past centuries when honoring other local historical events. Giosuè Carducci, the first Italian Nobel Laureate (1906), mentions it in his short poem *"On Marengo's fields"* celebrating the 1175 battle of Alessandria when the Lombardy League, an alliance of northern Italian cities backed by Pope Alexander III (who gave his name to Alessandria), defeated the army of the Holy Roman Emperor Frederick I Barbarossa. The rivers are also mentioned by the 19th-century poet and novelist Alessandro Manzoni, the author of the historical masterpiece *"The Betrothed"*. Manzoni's *"March 1821"* ode, exalting the first outbursts of *Risorgimento* in north-west Italy, the revolution that freed the Italian states from foreign domination and united them politically in a sole nation. He depicts the merging of the rivers lyrically as the marriage of the bride Bormida and the groom Tanaro. This wouldn't work in English where normally only human beings are referred to as male or female, with few exceptions – one being ships; in Italian and several other languages most nouns are treated as either feminine or masculine - or even neuter!

On 8 September 1943, a few weeks after the third anniversary of Italy's entering World War II, the provisional government empowered after Mussolini's deposition of 25 July announced it had signed an armistice with the Allies a few days before, and German forces took over northern and most of central Italy. Two days earlier, although these major developments were already on the horizon, nothing worrying was in the air yet around Alessandria and its rivers. On a clear sunny morning, one might have watched a man pulling a boat into the water from a patch of fine sand on the shore of the left bank of the "just married" Tanaro; it was a peculiar little rowing boat, a sort of skiff, looking odd there. The others, larger and bulky, moored to the trees along the river with long chains to allow for floods, were the pitch-coated, flat-bottomed crafts that had been used for centuries; they are steered by a man standing at the stern, with a long pole fitted with a sort of iron fork, at its flat side opposite the handle. The boatman propels the boat by plunging the pole into the water, at a suitable angle to the surface, until it hits the riverbed: then he pushes hard with both arms. Usually shallow water and a weak current make the job possible; occasionally, only in deeper waters, the pole is used as a paddle, secured or not to a sort of oarlock.

Swallows were flying high above the river, swooping in the crystal-clear September blue sky. The odd-looking little boat meanwhile had moved swiftly downstream gliding across the water in silence. The observer who might have seen it before at the beach, now from a distance would barely discern its "skinny" hull; but he wouldn't miss the wing-like rhythmic movement of the two long oars, looking a bit like those waterfowls that scuttle along in a long run before taking off. The man rowing had fitted a sliding seat facing the stern with his feet secured in a suitably distanced leg-stretcher; the boat was in fact partly equipped like a racing shell and years before Mario had been active in competitive sculling. He had learned the "anatomy" of a rowing stroke and was now showing it to his son Luciano, just eight that very day, who stayed put sitting at the stern, facing him - the boy had been warned not to stand up, otherwise the narrow-bottomed boat could capsize! A sculler begins with his arms fully extended holding the oars with their blades plunged at right angles into the water behind him, the legs bent and the seat at its closest point to the stern; then he slides backward by pushing with his legs and stretches his back towards the bow. Finally he completes the stroke by pulling the arms towards his chest till the oars' blades end up well in front of him. In the "recovery phase" of the stroke, the blades are lifted out of the water and rotated until they are parallel to it (this is referred to as "feathering" which, in Ernest Hemingway's magnificent novel "*A Farewell to Arms*", the main character Frederic, an experienced rower, names while escaping by boat to Switzerland via Lake Maggiore). Then they are brought back to the starting position and "squared" again, i.e. made perpendicular to the water to pull against it; meanwhile the rower on his seat moves back to his previous posture, close to the stern. Well-performed rowing with a sliding seat not only provides the most efficient man-powered propulsion of a floating object, but is an elegant, healthy, formative exercise involving most of the body muscles in full harmony.

So Mario rowed while looking forward to when his son would take his seat! In a few years the boy did just that, and became more and more familiar with the river and proficient in managing the craft; eventually, as he grew up, he even dared to challenge the floods for fun, for which his father severely upbraided him. The river had a long record of victims of drowning, mostly in the hot seasons when hapless locals who hardly knew how to swim went bathing.

On that September day either swimming in the river, which he loved doing when he reached his teens and later, or bravado-boating in flood-tides, did not even skim through Luciano's mind. He was excited about that Tanaro trip - he had been looking forward to it, and it was meant to be his father's birthday present - but his feelings were not altogether simply eager curiosity and pleasant surprise at the unprecedented happening. He enjoyed being on the boat when it started out swiftly from the shore and glided on the water like he had never experienced before; scaring a cormorant, whose take-off took a little time while it left behind a long, fast-fading wake on the glassy surface, and a little duck which dived right away, was also fun. Later on, though, he had a few worrisome moments.

Further downstream the Tanaro turned sharply to the right, after reaching the cliff-like south-east side of the hill with the castle on the top. As he got closer to the cliff side (on the left), Mario stopped rowing and showed his son there was no current: the boat stayed still - if anything it seemed to drift gently upstream. He explained they were floating over one of a sort of small pools where there is plenty of quite deep water (around 15 feet) all year around, even in the "dry" season when you could walk across the river bed at some points. Mario pointed out that these spots were a threat to bathers who were expected to know the river well and be good swimmers. Luciano couldn't swim and felt a bit uneasy there! The still boat was so close to the riverside that even when they looked up over the tips of a row of willows growing along the bank, the boaters could only see the sky, but when the craft drifted out a little, the trees no longer screened the dramatic view of the towering cliff and castle. The boy felt that the overhanging castle looked as if it were about to slide down into the river, and he didn't like that - it was frightening!

After a few hundred yards the river changed course again, curving gently to the left. On its left it now had a vast gravel shore where the water was so shallow that, even though it was cloudy, you could see the pebbles on the bottom. Further downstream a good deal of the river bed had dried up, leaving the left shore wider. The boat moved in closer to the fairly steep right bank, bordered first by large corn fields and further down by a plantation of poplars (for making paper). There the watercourse narrowed into a short tract of rapids which were easily manageable in the low-water season, when the current was sluggish and there were no obstacles. The swift boat ride through it was a bit bumpy that day, but Luciano once more found it fun.

The next, wider, slow-flowing section of the river was the home of the ferry. This consisted of two sturdy, tar-coated, wooden hulls about 20 yards long, held together by a central platform that could take two or even three ox- or horse-drawn carts. One bright-colored hut at each stern completed the craft, making it look friendly. The ferry was hooked onto a cable strung across the river and commuted between the two sides propelled solely by the current. Until the end of the 19th century, similar craft serving as mills could be seen along the main watercourses in northern Italy. The masterpiece "The mill on the Po", a historical novel by the outstanding 20th century writer Riccardo Bacchelli, dramatizes the saga of several generations of a family that owned a mill on the banks of the River Po, the biggest river in Italy (into which the Tanaro flows a few miles downstream from the ferry), against the background of Italy's political struggles from the time of Napoleon to the end of World War I.

Once they passed the ferry, Mario and his son had a good view of the township whose dwellings climb up to the castle along the gentle slope on the east side of the hill. In a few minutes they would be closer to their destination after another series of "slower" rapids ending in one more pool on the right side of the river; there, hidden by shrubbery, is the mouth of a creek which, according to popular myth, poured reddish water the day of the Marengo battle.

Having pulled the boat up onto a vast gravel bank on the opposite side of the river, they went walking, first rather uncomfortably - the boy had sandals on and felt the pebbles. A more walker-friendly trail in a poplar plantation followed but after a while the enjoyable stillness slowly surrendered to a puzzling distant noise. As father and son moved ahead it seemed there must be a lot of people talking and shouting, as if at a market, except that a variety of sharp, metallic sounds, like at a blacksmith's shop, contributed to the "concert". Luciano, whose Dad had not told him about their destination, felt more worried than curious, and in spite of his father turning to him and smiling silently several times, the boy didn't like to ask. A vast glade eventually opened up, revealing tens, probably not less than a hundred, partly wrecked motor vehicles of all sorts surrounded by an eager brigade busily taking them apart! The boy's stunned astonishment was short-lived because he was more interested in seeing what the cars he so loved - the real ones, not toys - were made of. His father gave him a short tour of the yard and some clue to how the various automobile parts the boy pointed at worked; he also explained those were mostly French non-combat military vehicles taken by the Italian Forces when they crossed the Alps into France shortly after the outburst of the war. For a short while this sort of junkyard had apparently been left unattended - and Luciano learned why in a couple of days!

Mario himself chose one of the cars where nobody else was busy, possibly a light Citroen truck, took some tools out of a cloth bag he had carried along and started to unscrew one of its wheels. He was almost half way through the job – he had cleared one of the two wheels he wanted to take away – when people came running into the glade, apparently from the nearby village, shouting: "The Germans! The Germans!". It was a stampede; everybody but Mario and his son rushed to hide, probably in a bushy area not too far away along the river. Then Mario dropped some tools he had not used from his bag, grasped one of his son's hands and, wielding a stick, started to move around slowly as if searching; "We are looking for snails" he said, turning to the speechless Luciano, who knew full well they are only found after the rain which had not fallen for months!

Neither Germans nor any other newcomers showed up; only the previous crowd returned quietly and resumed its endeavors as noisily as before. Mario too went back to "his" car to finish the job and cleared the other wheel. Carrying both of them down to the boat wasn't really hard along the poplars trail; they rolled straight and smoothly for up to 20 yards every time Mario launched one, to his son's amusement. Luciano wanted to try that himself but the result was unexpected. Understandably, the boy hadn't got his father's knack and strength and the wheel he tried to launch didn't even start straight and dropped right away under a bush alongside the trail, quite close to him. It so happened that, shortly before, a huge male pheasant feeding close to the trail had felt the father and son arriving and had hidden in that bush waiting for them to pass by – typical pheasant behavior! It hadn't counted on the wheel launched crookedly by the boy! You have to be familiar with the crashing sound of a male pheasant's take-off in the wild (something as shocking as

75

the unexpected shot of a firearm close by) to understand how the boy felt at the bird's escape: hail Nemesis! Having scared away a cormorant and a little duck on the water, Luciano was then frightened out of his wits by a different bird on land!

When the couple got back to the shore where they had left the boat it was about noon; the sun had warmed the pebbles, and the hot stones bothered Luciano more: he was also thirsty and couldn't find any fruit or drink in his father's bag. So Dad walked with him down to the edge of the pebbled shore and continued down a sandy bank towards the water. There, with his hands, he dug a kind of puddle in the soft soil just a span above the river surface: the cavity filled fast, first with muddy water, but it soon turned crystal clear as it gently poured out of the puddle. Mario reminded his thirsty son how to cup his hands like a bowl and.... that was it! In the 1970s the Tanaro topped the list of the most polluted Italian rivers; its pebbled shores had turned dark brown. Grown-up Luciano mentioned the puddle episode while lecturing on environmental devastation.

The boat advanced swiftly on the way home, even though it was going upstream; the two wheels it towed, just floating behind, looked like a tender. Back at the rapids upstream of the ferry, however, Mario preferred to walk through the shallow water, dragging the boat. Its usual mooring spot was about a hundred yards downstream from the sandy shore where they had started out earlier that morning. The bank there was quite sheer and Mario had carved several steps in it. As Luciano climbed up he hung on to the long chain secured to one of the willow trees whose drooping branches hid the boat which was also fastened to the chain. Mario took along the oars and the tiny sliding seat, but for the time being left the two wheels almost submerged and hardly visible, but it was just those wheels that troubled Luciano. His father, explaining while walking home, told him that in a devastated war and post-war economy those wheels were likely to prove a valuable item tradable with anything they might need. The boy in fact recalled being told by his mother that two people from Genoa had visited the village and traded salt (hard to come by in those days), homemade from sea water, for local farm produce. Even so Luciano, in a mental flashback to the incidents of that otherwise challenging and rewarding day, felt the stain of those wheels. He didn't dare tell his father or anybody else that he felt there was something wrong with taking them away, but he still thought so and never forgot the incident. Two days after that trip on the Tanaro, Mario unexpectedly found himself ferrying a few escaped Italian servicemen across the river in his tiny boat (no more than two at each crossing!). Although the ferry operated less than a mile away, it was safer for those men to keep as far as possible from roads, bridges and the like where they could encounter the wrong people - German forces who were taking control of northern and central Italy. To Luciano's and his family's surprise the fugitives had come at sunset from nearby Alessandria, where there were several barracks, a fortress, the star-shaped *Cittadella* (an impressive 18th-century masterpiece of military architecture) and other military installations. The men wore civilian clothes (they got more from Luciano's parents, with some food) and slept in the hayloft; they hoped to reach their homes, mostly far away in southern Italy. Luciano learned only years later about the events that led to their pitiful fate, but right away he felt sympathy for them and over the next few days he questioned his parents: would the fugitives ever make it home? Had they got children?

The events following the turn-round of July 25 that year, which empowered the provisional government of Marshal Pietro Badoglio, led to the worst of the conflict for Italy, with even greater hardship to the population: the country was split in two, each part fighting the other, and in one, the north, virtually under German occupation – an atrocious civil war loomed. After invading Sicily in July, the Allies crossed the Strait of Messina entering Calabria in southern Italy on 3 September; meanwhile their seaborne troops were landing on the neighboring coasts of the Campania (at Salerno just south of Naples) and Puglia regions (respectively the "shin" and "toe" of the boot-shaped Italian peninsula) where they took several ports including Brindisi. This was where King Victor Emmanuel III and his government, led by Marshal Badoglio had fled, fearing a German advance on Rome, just before their announcement of the armistice with the Allies on 8 September - with no prior notice to the Italian armed forces. Confusion reigned as the troops were left without orders: some promptly disbanded, hiding out like those showing up at Luciano's home, but most were caught and interned by the Germans who had been expecting Marshal Badoglio's government's *volte-face*. Part of the Italian armed forces' units which did not disband joined forces with the Germans against the Allies as before, but several other units refused and did not surrender. One tragic example was on the Greek island of Cephalonia where, in revenge, the Nazis executed five thousand of the nine thousand surviving Italian soldiers who had opposed them there.
The Commander-in-Chief of the German troops in Italy was General

Albert Kesselring, who earned the respect of his opponents, the Allies, for his military achievements, but could not evade blame for his troops' cruel retaliations on civilians. Luciano, early that September, read the General's unforgettable name on a leaflet dropped from the air which indeed warned than any harm suffered by his men while away from the front line would be cause for merciless retaliation against the population: hostages would be taken and executed if the actual culprit didn't show up.

Probably the first such episode occurred on 22 September in Palidoro near Rome: one German soldier was killed and another injured by an explosion while inspecting some boxes of ammunitions abandoned at the site. Their captain blamed the death on unnamed locals, demanded reprisal and arrested 22 farmers living in the area.

Sergeant Salvo D'Acquisto, the commander there of the Italian Carabinieri (the Kings's police), investigated the case and reported to the German captain that it was an accident and there had been no culprits. Since he was not believed, the hero confessed to being the culprit himself and traded his life for that of the hapless farmers. The Sergeant was awarded the gold medal for military valor and is now being evaluated for sanctification by the Catholic Church.

As German servicemen started to fall in ambushes by Italian partisans, the dreadful policy of Kesselring's threat was enacted. When 32 policemen marching through central Rome were killed by a bomb hidden in a trash can, 335 hostages including many Jews were taken, mostly civilians, Italian POWs and inmates from the town's prisons; they were executed and mass-buried on 24 March 1944 in a disused cement quarry near Ardeatina Street, hence the modern reference to the massacre as the *Fosse Ardeatine* (*fosse* meaning pits).

The worst of these events occurred between 29 September and 5 October 1944 around Marzabotto, a small village in the Apennine ridge south of Bologna. In reprisal for the locals' support to the partisans, the Nazis killed hundreds of people (728 according to their commander's official report). Victims included children, women, elderly persons and several Catholic priests.

Italians also suffered some atrocities from the Allies: during the invasion of Sicily, American troops under General George G. Patton (who reportedly in his rancorous briefings urged his men not to let the opponents surrender), in two separate incidents occurring at Biscari airfield between July and August 1943, murdered 74 Italian and two German POWs in cold blood. A British historian, James Holland, writing about the conduct of Allied corps in World War II in Italy, reckons they apparently looted more freely than the Germans; he also cites the appalling record of French Moroccan troops, who "raped their way through the mountains south of Rome without being held to account then or later".

Further major events in summer 1943, when the war spread on Italian soil, included the 12 September spectacular rescue of Mussolini by a German airborne commando unit (with no bloodshed) from captivity in a ski resort in the Apennine Mountains about 60 miles north-east of Rome: within two weeks he had set up a new Fascist state in North-Italy (RSI, *Repubblica Sociale Italiana*). Although often regarded as a puppet nation under German domination, the RSI spared the population a worse fate like that suffered by the Nazi-oppressed Poles and assured decent basic public services like pension payments and mail services (issuing new stamps), though at dire cost. The RSI armed forces, GNR (*Guardia Nazionale Repubblicana*), generally distrusted by the Germans when they joined them against the Allies, were occasionally engaged in fratricidal combat with the partisans (sometimes even members of the same family took opposite sides!). However, this mostly involved a special corps, the *Brigate Nere* (Black Brigades), who were trained specifically for that purpose: everybody blamed them for being poorly disciplined. The Italian Jews who until then had mostly managed to escape the worst threats, because of the fairly bland application of Fascist racial laws, were then fully exposed to the risk of deportation to the Nazi camps in Germany. On 16 October Rome witnessed the shocking Ghetto Roundup of over one thousand Jews for the gas chambers of Auschwitz.

Meanwhile in the southern parts of the country, where the Allies' advance was being efficiently checked by Kesselring's limited forces since he had planned well in anticipation of a 'blow to the shin' (the American 5th Army entered Naples only on 1 October), the King chose Brindisi as the site for the Marshal Badoglio's government and eventually declared war on Germany on 13 October. Sadly, that meant that young Italians wearing different uniforms were going to clash on the firing line and kill each other.

The most shameful pages of his home country's 20th-century history were just turning over when Luciano entered his eighth year. The boy's interest and understanding of those times was gradually maturing, but the limited events he had witnessed or perceived listening to adults did not yet tell him enough about that war and the many facets of its atrocities. The worst still lurked and Luciano was meant to face situations that turned boys into men faster: some only a few years older than him sadly did so too fast and traded their toy weapons dreadfully for the real thing.

10. Life in the Countryside

Virgil, one of the foremost Latin poets, is best known as the author of the Aeneid, which tells of the myth of the Trojans who survived defeat by the Greeks and traveled to Italy to become progenitors of the ancient Romans. He is also prized for his poem The Georgics (from the Greek, "On Working the Earth") which deals with farming methods, like raising crops, plants and livestock. When Luciano's parents found shelter in their ancestors' village Pietra Marazzi, throughout the last two and a half years of the second world conflict, the boy witnessed a lot of hard rural work still involving fairly primitive methods not unlike those portrayed poetically by Virgil. At that time he had already had some experience of life in the countryside, although only for a short time, when he was three years younger. Beside grandmother Giuseppina's poultry he had seen the farm workers threshing wheat just before he listened in the village to the public broadcast of Mussolini's epochal speech.

Threshing wheat and pressing the straw into bales were the only jobs done with the aid of machines powered by a steam engine. These horse-drawn implements were brought to the village for a few days each year. A huge belt some 15 ft long transmitted motion from the engine to the thresher and another, similar, from the latter to the straw press. The revolving belts, which in these fairly remote settings lacked the most basic safety measures, were a feared source of danger, to be kept at a respectful distance, though even so now and then not enough! For any other heavy farming tasks requiring power, only oxen were used and in country households every child was assigned chores.

Luciano returned to Pietra from Belluno in 1943, presumably in early August, well after the wheat harvest and threshing, but still in time to play a small role in the corn harvest shortly after. Corn fields abounded in the plains around the village and the Mensi family had sown at least one that year. Giovanni Mensi, no relation to

Giuseppina, lived in a small farmstead across the street to the rear of Luciano's home, with his wife Ester and four children including Luigi who was shortly to attend school with Luciano in third grade. Several weeks before the harvest farmers, to expose the lower-growing ears of corn to more sunlight, used to cut the upper portion (about 2 ft) of the tall stems, which on average were 7-10 ft high. Hand harvesting involved detaching the ripe, dry ears of corn, i.e. the cobs still tightly wrapped in several layers of leaves, from the stalk. Everything else, i.e. the stovers, was saved for livestock feed, while the cobs were collected for threshing.

Luciano didn't join the Mensi harvest, but later on helped further with the cobs they took home in preparation for threshing: the tight foliage wrapping each cob had to be removed by hand. These husks were then piled up in the courtyard after dinner, in the evening, when the heat of the day was abating. This gave an opportunity for a sort of get-together since generally neighbors and other villagers joined the household as harvest helpers. Boys and girls were welcome and allowed to stay up late because school was still closed: singing, jokes and story-telling were the usual entertainment.

Luciano at the time was not interested in other sidelines and saved no memories about some of the young folks ... "courting on the sly'", which was quite likely while it was getting dark, as depicted by the main character and narrator in Mark Twain's 19th-century novel '*The Adventures of Huckleberry Finn*', written with much U.S. southern twang. From the older farmers the boy learned that they used to save the husks from 'unwrapping' the cobs for stuffing mattresses. Next came preparing the threshing floor where the corn kernels (grains) from the thresher were laid out to dry in the sun; grandfather Joe's large courtyard was probably one or the few concrete-paved ones and only needed a quick wash to prevent the threshed corn spoiling by getting mixed with dust and debris. Otherwise the farmers would sweep their turf yard with a broom and "cure" it by spraying a loose slurry made by stirring cow dung in plenty of water - that came as quite a surprise to Luciano! He remembers that the village tinsmith operated a threshing machine powered by a small diesel engine. He must have seen it working in Joe's courtyard, whose corn harvest was no doubt several times larger than the Mensi's; they probably didn't need anything more than their own hand-turned thresher. Other villagers beside the tinsmith earned a living from more than one job. Mr. Cacciola, who on Sunday morning and some other days opened his barbershop (the only one in Pietra), also had a corn mill.

82

It was customary to eat freshly-milled newly-harvested corn in the dish called *polenta*, obtained by patiently stirring - continuously for not less than 50 min - corn flour poured little by little into boiling water in a sort of inverted-bell-shaped copper pot known as a *paiolo,* to obtain a really smooth, creamy texture.True *polenta* (ready-made and fast food versions are available now) is still a classic throughout northern Italy in the third millennium; it is served as a gourmet dish, enriched with wild mushrooms, game, or *gorgonzola* cheese, in high-end restaurants. However, in the years when corn imported from the New World was preferred for its yields and prevailed over the other cereals, polenta (or other corn-based foods) was eaten regularly in several poor regions and became a major part of the diet needed to satisfy a worker's energy and nutrient requirements. But *polenta* lacked some of the nutrients essential for well-being (like the vitamin niacin and the key amino acids tryptophan and lysine - a deficit that was not discovered for a long time). So a serious disease of malnutrition, pellagra, was widespread in Europe right up into the 20th century and occurred also in the in the U.S. south.

The other harvest Luciano became familiar with was the vintage. Most of the cultivable lands of the gentle hills overlooking Pietra Marazzi were vineyards and in September the village was lively as at no other time in the year. The event involved almost all the locals and many would join in from elsewhere to help. People were bustling round like ants making an anthill. The various tasks included repairing and cleaning the wooden casks and the wine press in the cellars; fitting the big tub-like wooden tanks for collecting and crushing grapes onto oxen-drawn carts; commuting to and from the vineyards crowded with harvesters. Vintage was in the air and as the first winemaking started, you could smell it even from a distance! Since any quick burst of bad weather could spoil the harvest, once grapes were ripe they all had to be picked by hand – many hands - with the least possible delay. Joe's vineyard covered a vast south-looking square area on a slight slope and was by far the village's biggest. On either side of the broad driveway running several hundred yards up the hill in the middle of the groves, dozens of parallel rows of vines stretched away at right angles. The layout was designed so that for most of the day the vines in any row were least shaded by those above and below them. Only a few old cherry trees had been spared when Joe had set out that vineyard on his return from Tennessee. It was planted with almost all the same variety of vines, producing wine grapes, although white table grapes could be spotted too. Thus when Luciano visited the vineyard at the right time with his cousin Gabriele, they used to help themselves to those delicious fruits. As long as the boys broke off a whole cluster of grapes from a vine and ate them, like Joe recommended, that was all right. But they had the bad habit of picking only a few berries from different clusters here and there while walking through the rows. That upset Joe who regarded the place as a garden and couldn't stand even a single spoiled fruit. There was not enough room between the rows for the carts carrying the tanks, so they waited in the driveway. The harvesters picking the grapes, generally women and kids, saved them in baskets to be loaded onto the carts - a man's job as a rule. Rather than carrying the actual baskets, though, the men (if sturdy enough) found it more convenient to use a typical large container, the *brenta,* which they strapped on their backs like a huge knapsack. It was made of thin wooden staves about 4 ft long bound with hoops, narrowing its more or less oval cross-section from the wide-open top end to the half-sized closed one at the bottom. The *brenta* was also referred to as a capacity unit (about 20 gallons, or 75 liters) and could be used during winemaking as a decanter to transfer fermented must into a different vessel.

Driving the loaded carts downhill back to the village was quite an art. Joe, who kept an eye on everything, warned his men against overloading. He also shouted to keep away the kids who, like Luciano, had been allowed a trip on the carts on the way up. Those poorly-braked vehicles were ill suited for slopes; their wheels could not be slowed down to an appropriate speed, but could only be blocked, so they slithered on the steepest roads, this being the only option. When that happened the carts tended to slide dangerously toward one side rather than go forward, a prelude to capsizing!

Vineyards have to be attended properly almost all year round. This includes frequent weeding, turning over the soil and smoothing out the ground, pruning the vines, leaving only some shoots, shaped by securing them to the frames along the rows, spraying the leaves with copper sulphate and the flowers with sulphur, to prevent fungal parasites. Towards the end of the war, it was hard to find copper sulphate but since the Italian penny (one cent of the Lira - the currency at the time) was worth nothing and some villagers could get hold of sulfuric acid, they used to mix it with the copper coins to make the missing stuff.

The curious story of how copper sulphate protected the vines Luciano learned from the Boys' Encyclopedia, which he could consult thanks to his friend Doctor Carlo. A French botany professor in Bordeaux had noticed how the vines closest to the roads were spared from fungal infection and found they had been sprayed with a mixture of copper sulphate and hydrated lime (still used and called Bordeaux mixture), intended to deter passers-by from eating the grapes, which then tasted bitter (and stained the culprits' hands!).

In the late 19th century almost all European vineyards were destroyed by a mysterious pest and it took decades for wine production to recover. In France desperate peasants abandoned their devastated vineyards and left their homes. It turned out that a tiny deadly insect, the phylloxera, accidentally imported from the New World with some vines, fed on the plant roots and leaves, leaving scars that opened the way to fungal infections. The problem was eventually solved by grafting cuttings of the prized Old World vine varieties onto resistant American rootstock. The accidental discovery of the antifungal properties of copper helped too.

The wine was actually made in the village; the carts carrying the tanks full of grapes were parked at the entrance to the cellars and grapes were traditionally crushed by trampling them barefoot. For red wines everything (the sugar-rich juice plus the woody parts of the grapes such as stems and seeds) was poured into the primary fermentation vessels from the *brentas*. Then only the free-running wine was transferred to other vessels (the best were oak casks) for secondary fermentation and aging for weeks, months or even years. The residues - skin, stems and stalks - were pressed to obtain a lesser-quality wine: what was left after pressing, known as pomace, was sold to distillers to make *grappa*. This is a uniquely Italian strong crystal-clear liqueur (up to 60% alcohol by volume, 120 US proof) with grape fragrance. Top connoisseur brands are distilled from selected pomace of a single grape variety, especially *Nebiolo*, used to make some of the finest Piedmont wines - *Barolo*, *Barbaresco* and *Gattinara*. Because of the abundance of the woody parts of the grapes in pomace, distillation produces not only ethanol but also the highly toxic wood alcohol (methanol) which must be discarded - as only skilled and careful licensed *grappa* makers do. This is why under Italian law winemakers are required to sell pomace only to authorized distillers, and home distillation is prohibited. Was there any moonshine *grappa* in Pietra Marazzi? Luciano never heard about it, but the peasants' creativity, sharpened by the scarcity of so many items in wartime, was most probably not applied only to work (like for copper sulphate) but fun too!

The grape harvest, lasting up to the first days of November

depending on the weather, was the last important field event after wheat and corn. There was a large sugar manufacturing plant in nearby Marengo (the grand-daughters of the boss there, Nevine and Ivonnette, whose mother was Belgian, were Luciano's schoolmates), but sugar beet was only a marginal crop - if any - in Pietra in the early 1940s.

Farming in the fall mostly involved preparing the fields for sowing which implied ploughing the soil and spreading fertilizers, then mostly organic, meaning animal manure and urine mixed with soiled bedding straw, with a contribution of household excreta (there were squat-toilets outside in huts close to the stable and their sewage was collected in the tank used for livestock refuse). Thus when the peasants started to enrich their fields with the appropriate nutrients, there was once again something in the air one could smell from a distance, though not as inspiring as at the grape harvest!

In the cold season the stables, especially those in the middle of the village next to their owners' houses like Joe's, hosted after-dinner meetings enjoyed by quite a few city folk too, who had moved temporarily to the village because of the war. Those hard times made it easy for peasants to 'socialize' with newcomers with quite different backgrounds, particularly the young people. Giuseppe Suppa, Nevine's and Ivonnette's teenage brother, was among the exotic guests. Luciano never attended those gatherings which lasted well beyond his bed-time, though he may have met Giuseppe elsewhere – he actually did two decades later when they were both working in the Milan medical school. It was cousin Gabriele, who lived with Joe, who described the stable meetings to Luciano. They were something similar to those where corn cobs were "unwrapped" before threshing, and involved the same sort of social interactions.

Since the stable guests were not busy with any chore - certainly not helping with corn cobs - everything involved some form of entertainment. One was playing cards; Joe excelled at *Briscola*, probably Italy's most popular card game requiring memory and tactics more than gambling skills. He was virtually unbeatable and Gabriele joined him as his partner in games of two teams. According to Luciano's cousin he and grandfather exchanged information on each other's cards, usually with silent signs, typically winking. Giuseppe played the harmonica, reportedly rather well and that, according to Gabriele, also helped with the "chicks" in the party (Luciano's cousin had to explain he didn't mean poultry!). However, the card-playing corner was the best-lit angle in the stable and when Giuseppe happened to try card-gaming in partnership, his slight tic, a frequent wink, showed up. What a shame: it sent the wrong signals to his partner and was not so attractive to the girls!

Early in the cold season was also the time for slaughtering the pigs; at least two men (the butcher was one) were needed to immobilize an animal with its legs tied across its chest. Heedless of the pig's pathetic squeals, they stretched its neck and exposed the throat to a sharp knife cut from which blood gushed unstoppably until death followed, after a minute of trumpeting calls for mercy.
The next year that cruel fate struck one of the pigs raised in Luciano's household (the other was sold); the boy was at school so he was spared the cruel sight. However, on returning home, he witnessed a good deal of the butcher's work. Almost all of a pig, including its trotters, can be used as food. Preparation of bacon, ham, salami and sausages is mostly done by curing with salt to preserve them. Traditionally sausages were made of tissues and organs that are perfectly edible and healthy, but not very appealing, such as scraps and cuttings, organ meats, blood, and fat; everything was ground and filled into a tubular casing, made from the cleaned intestine, turned inside-out. Lard was rendered by heating fatty tissue bits - small scraps of fried meat, skin, or membrane - in a pan, giving a product known in America as *cracklings*, which were Luciano's delight. Typical Italian pork cold meats are *lardo*, made by curing strips of fat with rosemary and other herbs and spices, and *prosciutto* – ham – which is the salt-cured meat from a pig's leg.
Processing pork products was one more way of preserving food that Luciano learned about in those war years weathered much better in rural settings where people wisely hoarded their harvest: was that what Virgil meant almost two thousand years earlier?

> Oh! all too happy tillers of the soil,
> Could they but know their blessedness, for whom
> Far from the clash of arms all-equal earth
> Pours from the ground herself their easy fare!

The boy's household stored fruit and vegetables too. Homemade fruit preserves were a family tradition in Pietra. In addition Giuseppina used to dry plums and sliced apples in the sun; the process first troubled her grandson when he saw they were covered with a blanket of flies and other insects. However, he was reassured when the large iron trays borrowed from the public bakery and containing the drying fruits were taken back there and placed in the oven for a while. As regards vegetables, large supplies of tomatoes were boiled down to a thick sauce, then bottled like wine (but with the addition of sodium salicylate as preservative: eating pasta with that sauce was like taking an aspirin!). The bottles were best stored in a cool place. One evening Luciano's mother, planning to do some cooking the next day, unwisely left two bottles too close to the stove. The following morning the red stuff had burst out all over, leaving two big, distinctive spots on the ceiling!

Growing up in the countryside in those days left Luciano's personality with an indelible major trait that outlasted and even thwarted many other formative events in his life, enjoyable and not. Never mind that throughout his adult life he had tasted many sophisticated settings - and at times found them hard to bear - the once country boy remained hopelessly a proudly happy bumpkin!

11. White Christmas

The winter of 1943 happened to be really cold in Pietra Marazzi. One day in December, Luciano's Dad took him to the river without carrying along the oars and didn't look long at their boat; he already knew it had been seriously damaged by gunfire from the opposite bank of the River Tanaro. Most probably a unit of the detested *Brigate Nere* (Black Brigades), the Fascist paramilitary groups that had been operating in northern Italy from the second half of that year, had been trying out their weapons. What Mario did carry on that trip, however, was a pair of ice skates. The Tanaro, in fact, was almost completely frozen with only a narrow stream of running water in mid-course, where the ice came out from the shore on both sides and almost joined. However, Mario and his son went some hundred yards upstream from where the boat was moored and there a minor branch of the river, after splitting further upstream - next to the confluence with the Bormida - merged back into the main watercourse. That was known as the *Tanaro morto* (dead) because it only had water in it at times like the spring or fall floods. That day, however, midway to the confluence there was just a frozen pond, making a natty small skating rink. Mario was a fairly good skier and while in Belluno hadn't missed an opportunity to enjoy the renowned Faloria *pistes*, the slopes in nearby Cortina. But when it came to ice skating, probably he had never tried before. Still, with his son insisting, he eventually took a chance. The story goes that some time earlier Luciano had happened on those strange items of footwear - the skates - and asked his Dad about them. He learned what they were meant for and couldn't wait to see a demo. Mario had brought those skates back from Russia and there was a lot more to them than meets the eye!

The boy listened eagerly when Dad recounted his war memories, generally limited to curious non-scary episodes; the horrors and cruelties he discovered years later, often when leafing through the photos Mario had shot with his personal Leica. One shows rows of supposedly Italian servicemen's frozen corpses laid out in the snow in the middle of nowhere: just a single rough wooden cross stands as the only collective token of mourning. Another shot portrays an endless multitude of unkempt troops clumsily marching; their route stretches to the horizon in an uneven white expanse under gloomy skies; only a few man-drawn sleighs can be seen carrying some of their disabled companions (frostbite!).

While reporting his recollections of the Russian front, Luciano's dad never mentioned the episodes involving his own bold, fearless behavior but he did tell of some of the tricks he and his associates - like other crews of cameramen - used to make their reportages seem more dramatic without running any additional risk. For example, they would bury explosive charges scattered over a large area, each connected to a fuse of a different length so that a sequence of explosions could be set off and filmed, then shown as resulting from an enemy air raid or artillery bombing.

The Russian front line stretched for about 15 hundred miles from the Baltic to the Black Sea. Mario, because of his job as a LUCE war correspondent embedded in the ARMIR (Italian Army in Russia), was constantly moving across the German and Italian lines. In mid-1942 the latter (about 250 thousand troops) were mostly positioned for over 100 miles along the River Don's northern bend. It was hardly likely that Mario might by chance bump into anybody he knew. Yet on settling briefly in Millerovo (Rostov Province) he noticed a towering aerial in the town's section hosting the Italians' quarters; it belonged to a mobile military radio station that he reckoned was worth filming. Oddly enough, a young telegraph operator, the parish's sharecropper's son from Pietra, 20- year-old Francesco Cervetti, had been assigned there. You can imagine the astonishment - and touching feeling of homesickness - of the two men finding themselves accidentally together so far away from their home village of about 400 souls. Cesco, as he was known, also witnessed the Russian air raid on Millerovo which could have cost Mario his life had he not left his barrack at the last minute. What Cesco saw when visiting the place after the raid, was a huge crater carving into half of Mario's room's floor; an unexploded half-buried bomb had swept down a carpet and some furniture including the table where he had just ended writing home; incredibly, the spared - though crumpled - stationery did reach his loved ones.

Mario during his war assignment met a few more fellow Italians he knew were there, whose whereabouts he could find out, the last one under tragic circumstances the following year, not long before the ruinous retreat of the ARMIR from Russia. The third winter had witnessed the critical turning situation of the Italian troops along the Don, especially after overwhelming Soviet forces backed by T-34 tanks and fighter-bombers defeated first the weak Romanian and Hungarian units positioned on the right and the left of the Italians respectively. By the end of January 1943, despite the heroic conduct of many - particularly the Alpini troops (Italian Mountain Corps) - the same fate befell the ARMIR. Appalling figures in the records illustrate the carnage when 130,000 Italians were surrounded by the Soviets: 20,800 died in combat, 64,000 were captured, and only 45,000 managed to withdraw.

It must have been early in January that Mario set out in search of his best friend who he wanted to rescue. With Aldo Ravasi, a notary and an Alpine Mountain Corps captain, he had shared the best years of their youth in Pietra, from Jole's parties at the Castle to boating on the river. Mario, who had a good car and enough fuel to drive far enough from the impending Russian advance, which could hardly be opposed, was well informed through his frequent encounters with high-ranking commanders, about the war's developments and quite reasonably he fretted about Aldo's fate. But the captain, who had lost his parents when a child and was still single, didn't listen to his friend's advice to leave together: "You've got a family at home, you go. My family is here: I'll never leave them." Aldo was never heard of again. The day Mario walked down to the Tanaro with his son to try the Russian ice skates, and passed the boat he had shared so often with his friend, the captain's last words must have resounded once more loud and clear in his mind.

During his adventurous retreat, Mario further experienced the friendly, humane attitude and hospitality of the Russian country folk, even more then as a fugitive invader. They lived in farmsteads called *izbas*, log houses built with simple tools such as axes, spades, knives and ropes. A constant feature of an *izba* was the Russian stove, a home-heating device designed to retain heat for long periods, something like the Cadorine stoves fitted in the apartment in Belluno, where Mario's family was awaiting his return. People could sleep on the top of the stove to keep warm and in fact Mario did just that several times, as the only guest. He later reported he hadn't worried much because he was so desperately tired and cold, but he could in fact have easily been killed while sleeping there.

Plenty of snow fell in Pietra Marazzi that winter; Luciano could sport his little sleigh Dad had brought him back from Belluno, while his pals were struggling with roughish home-made ones or other unwieldy substitutes like washboards. Sunny days, however, were not so frequent. There was fog in winter too, though not as often as in autumn, and it hid the castle topping the eastern hill. That offered a fairy-tale view when the imposing building faded away into the mist or drifted back out from it; the snowy landscape added to the enchantment.

Thus for Luciano the cold season meant staying indoors more, spending his spare time there after finishing homework. Gianni, a schoolmate, visited regularly him and the two played with toy soldiers or with cars that the boys pretended were racing on a speedway. Yet something that really moved, even if slowly, was under construction, following directions from the Boys' Encyclopedia. A wooden spool without any thread (the kind mother used in her sewing machine) was first fitted with a tiny rubber band passed through its hole and secured at one end with a little stick, about as wide as its diameter, which could not turn. A wax disk about quarter of an inch thick, consisting of a slice of candle, was cut to fit onto the other end of the spool. The rubber band was passed out through a hole in this disk and secured with another stick, with a short part fitted into a groove carved into the wax; the other part, several times longer, served like a handle to turn the wax disk and wind up the rubber band. Once the spool was placed with both rims and the longer stick's edge on a flat surface, it turned and moved forward, propelled by the stretched rubber band as it unwound. When Gianni and Luciano each had one of these "handicrafts", they ran two kinds of competition. In one, on the "speedway" - the kitchen table - the winner was the one whose "car" was first to cross the finishing line; in the other, the "Sahara Desert" - the kitchen floor - the score was the distance the toy covered till its "rubber power" ran out. It took quite a while and some struggling before the boys could get their "spool cars" to work satisfactorily, but even then the game didn't last longer than any other, as they got bored with it sooner or later. Ironically the only evergreen amusements while the tragedy of the second world conflict unfolded, seemed to involve toy weapons - though now and then even real ones! As reported to Luciano by his cousin Gabriele, one day Gianni showed up with a revolver, presumably belonging to his grandfather, and greatly excited a bunch of his peers. That didn't go unnoticed by some older youths passing by who asked him to hand over the weapon; they claimed they only wanted to stop the boy harming himself. But Gianni kept the intruders at gunpoint and later on went to hide that handgun with Gabriele. Gianni, who never mentioned the event to Luciano, had come to the village from Genoa, lived with his grandparents, and was considered a difficult boy. However, Luciano's household welcomed him and when he was there he never fell short of what they expected from a desirable guest.

That snowy winter of 1943 just called out for a white Christmas. Luciano, like his peers, was looking forward to the arrival of Baby Jesus (or rather to the toys he hoped for!). At that time Italian boys and girls used to write directly to him, asking for the gifts they dreamed of. Father Christmas or Santa Claus were not known and nor were Christmas trees; they came only later on, after the war, together with Coca-Cola and chewing gum! During the Christmas season a nativity scene, called a *presepe* or *presepio*, was set up in homes and churches; it consisted of figurines assembled to depict the infant Jesus lying in a manger and attended by Mary and Joseph; other statuettes and handicrafts represented those who went to revere the newborn Messiah in a stable and its humble surroundings. The presepio's tradition goes back to the Middle Ages when Saint Francis of Assisi first staged a sort of pantomime displaying a nativity scene, after visiting the Holy Land where he had been shown Jesus' traditional birthplace. The static nativity scenes came later on, including modest home-made ones as well as some artistic masterpieces. The presepio's main features are based on the accounts of Jesus' birth in the Gospels of Matthew or Luke. Mary and Joseph traveled to Bethlehem for the census and, obliged by necessity to stay in a stable instead of an inn, placed the newborn in a manger. An angel announced the birth of Jesus to the shepherds who came to worship him. The *Magi* – the three Kings, or three wise men – followed from afar some time after Jesus' birth, led by a star. Customary additions to the nativity scenes, not mentioned in either Gospel, include an ox and ass in the stable as well as other animals, such as sheep, goats and camels in the surroundings; people engaged in different trades are also shown. Usually a comet hangs above the stable, although astronomers' attempts to identify a specific event in the heavens accounting for the star mentioned in the Gospel of Matthew have been unsuccessful. Of course the household's juniors enjoyed being involved in setting up the presepio and Luciano had an opportunity to prove his creativity; the round mirror his dad used to shave made a fine pond in the nativity display, though more like a frozen one, like where he had tried the Russian ice skates.

Whether anyone beside Luciano also noticed that the mirror was the very one that had reflected his disheveled appearance just after he had escaped serious harm from playing with gunpowder, is not known; in that respect the boy's presepe's pond might well have served as a votive token to Baby Jesus!

12. The Soundtrack of the War

Besides his exchanges with the flip book and gunpowder, Luciano wangled another barter with cousin Gabriele to get hold of a short-cut made up of a few frames of a motion picture film. The boy intended to assemble a magic lantern - one more suggestion from the Boys' Encyclopedia. As it happened, he didn't actually get any further than a rough prototype, i.e. a piece of cardboard, the size of a tabloid newspaper page, fitted with a lens in the middle and bent twice at the two sides so it could stand on a bedside table, facing the wall which likewise was shaded from the direct light of the table lamp. By working out the right point (between the lens and the lamp, though much closer to the former) where a frame ought to be held, Luciano could "project" a just-about-sharp-enough image onto the wall; this taught him that the film image turned upside down when passing through the lens! But that was not all. After a really close look at his bit of film, he noticed an additional feature besides the frames and the perforations he knew served for the gear advancing it: a thin, jiggling strip along one side. That was for Luciano's dad to explain; these strips, he told his son, stored (as a means of light modulation) a movie's dialogue, music and noises: in a word it was the soundtrack. Nowadays cinema is becoming digital and motion picture film and its reels will soon be only obsolete collectors' items.

Luciano's memories of the war years, like a movie - albeit an old one with all the faults of aging - included some sort of soundtrack, although the way the human brain stores (and retrieves) information is a lot more complex and still largely unknown, compared to any man-made audio or video recording devices. But those records, particularly the less recent ones like those relying on film, wear out with repeated playing and lose quality, eventually becoming totally erased. Human long-term memories, in contrast, are best preserved in people who like to think over past events often; Luciano's imaginative tendencies from an early age fit in with this line of thought.

To begin with there were his recollections of war noises, the worst being the smash and rumble of an aeroplane and the burst of machine gun fire as if it dived onto his home. Luckily this memory didn't last too long, though it was frightening enough. That night, even before the suddenly awakened, stunned boy could ask for help, Dad rushed to his bed where he found him shaking uncontrollably. The worried man had never seen anything like that. What could he know about the extent to which a sudden, emotionally triggered surge of the hormone adrenaline in the blood dramatically alters body functions in order to put it into "protective" mode? He couldn't stop his son shaking and just when it looked as if the tremors were getting weaker, at a further low-flying passing of that darned plane Luciano started again.

For some time after that he would wake up during the night as if dreaming about it, but that plane - or any other at bed-time - which had caused nothing more serious than panic in the village, never showed up again. However, in late 1943 and in 1944, similar low-altitude night air raids, mostly involving a single plane and often causing no or only limited civilian damage, were widely reported in northern Italy. Thus in popular lore a mythical, nocturnal plane - though the episodes were real - became known as "*Pippo*". It is not really clear where it got this name, but the funny Disney character Goofy, known as *Pippo* in Italy, is one candidate. Otherwise a popular Italian song of the Thirties describes a dandy named *Pippo* who strolls through town convinced he is a model of handsomeness and elegance, whereas people laugh at his labored outfits. In either case it would seem that those who weathered the mysterious plane's intrusions wanted to exorcise their fear by trying to make fun of it. Several decades later the mystery was largely unravelled: the British RAF had carried out a special two-fold project based on the guidelines of psychological warfare. It involved disturbing the prevailing night traffic by any route - the only possible one because of the intense day-long air raids by U.S. planes - by flying about a dozen fast aircraft to raid most of northern Italy nightly. That hampered travel and transport, including deliveries to the front line; at the same time it scared the population in an attempt to break the enemy's morale.

The first airborne ground-scanning radar system designed to identify fixed and moving targets for night and all-weather flying was essential to accomplish these missions, which relied on the high-performing de Havilland DH 98 aircraft known as the Mosquito. Ironically,

immediately after the war Moto Garelli of Milan began production of a cycle motor, the Mosquito 38A, a little power unit that could be fitted in a few minutes to any standard bicycle. It was to be Luciano's first "racing motorbike" (top speed 20 mph) that he flaunted when he was about twelve - and much bolder than that infamous night!.
Dreadful daytime air raids by the Allies' low-flying aviation targeted anything, although usually sparing civilians. Luciano witnessed one such attack, but hardly panicked that time. One afternoon a fast plane dived in front of the house, heading towards the river, and a passing cyclist hastily dived to hide in the ditch along the roadside. But the air attack targeted the ferry at Montecastello, out of sight on the other side of the eastern hill, so the machine gun's deadly noise was heavily muffled. One of the two hulls was badly damaged, but the craft didn't sink and the boatman attending it suffered only minor injuries.

Luciano also became acquainted with the unmistakable noise of military small arms fire, notably the bursts of automatic rifles – those that discharged multiple shots in close sequences (at rates of several hundreds per minute). Regardless of the number of shots, each single one's pitch was substantially higher and much shorter-lasting than that of the ordinary two-barrel 12-gauge shotgun the boy was already familiar with. Several villagers, in fact, were fervent hunters – Luciano dreamed of becoming one some day. He first experienced an automatic rifle's burst while with his father, climbing a narrow trail on the steep southward-looking side of the hill topped by the castle. A young man in his Black Brigades uniform, hardly out of his teens (his family name was Sassi and probably they lived in the castle's burg) who was walking along the road beside the river bank, fired his weapon into the air. The boy had mixed feelings, but fear prevailed over his keen interest in firearms. Dad encouraged him by explaining that the young soldier, down there alone, was probably frightened himself and was just trying to overcome his insecurity.
The same militiaman showed up at the village some time afterwards and Luciano eagerly enjoyed a close, probing look at his MAB 38 A gun (*Moschetto Automatico Beretta 1938*), made by Pietro Beretta of Brescia, one of the world oldest-established (1526) family firms. It could be recognized by its wooden stock and perforated cooling sleeve over the barrel. The MAB is widely acknowledged as the most successful and effective Italian small arm of World War II; however, it required extensive craft work to be fine-tuned and made reliable. Thus, because of limited production, the number needed became vailable only in the last years of the conflict. After the war ended

Luciano got a close look at the British Sten, another legendary small arm of the time. It was made of simple, stamped metal components requiring minimum manufacturing and could be finished with a few man-hours of work. Its distinctive 'bare-look' features were a metal loop as stock and a horizontal magazine. Stens parachuted to the Italian partisans by the Allies contributed substantially to their weaponry.

World War II handguns were similarly appealing to Luciano and most of his peers, first of all the awful, mythical German Luger P 08, readily identified by its exposed barrel, breech assembly's knee joint and curved butt. Oddly, in those years the boys' craze for those deadly objects was not limited by their actually having witnessed the evil they caused.

A typical scary noise of those times that Luciano, however, hardly recalls hearing - if at all - was the civil defence sirens to warn of air raids. There must have been several in Alessandria, but the hills sheltering Pietra Marazzi from them stopped their sound reaching the village. He could still hear the explosions caused by the Allies' heavy bombing raids on Alessandria, about six miles away from the opposite side of the western hill, though it was somehow dulled, like far-off thunderstorms. Because he had only a vague idea of the devastation involved, particularly the human lives lost, and since he had been reassured that the enemy would never deem the village worth its annihilating air power, at first he hardly worried. But he was surely shocked the day his mother, still with messy, dusty hair and clothes, came back from town after miraculously surviving one of those raids (and later, unseen, he eavesdropped on her frightening report). She had gone to Alessandria to pick up some items from the flat where the family planned to live after the war, and arranged that a man with his horse-drawn cart would help do the job. A bomb reduced the building on the other side of the street to rubble, while Mother and other bystanders had just rushed into the basement set up as an air raid shelter. The poor horse, still hooked up to the carriage blocked in the courtyard, thankfully came through unharmed too - but wouldn't stop neighing for help.

The radio, a five-tube superheterodyne top-notch receiver Dad had brought from Belluno, fairly free of interfering noise and crackling (except for the short waves, which Luciano hardly knew existed at the time), was a blessed indoor resource for the whole family. Mother kept it on all day long while working through her household chores and

Luciano eagerly listened to anything broadcast by the EIAR (*Ente Nazionale Radiofonico Italiano*), the Italian state radio. Beside the censored news, it offered entertainment like different kinds of music, especially patriotic and war songs. Luciano's favorite was the "Submariners' Hymn" exalting the courage of those who dared to challenge the enemy from unplumbed depths. Mother preferred the more enticing ones, such as the funny tunes sung by Natalino Otto. His vast repertoire included one called *Pippo*, which might possibly have inspired the nickname for the scary nightime British air raids. His singing style had strong American influences (jazz and swing) whose forerunners Mother had met on the Mississippi riverboats as a little girl. Mr. Otto was a Genovese who in 1935 had performed for an Italian-American radio station in New York City. Back in Italy he joined up with two great Italian bandleaders, Gorni Kramer and Pippo Barzizza. The latter - known personally to Luciano's grandmother Giuseppina - was from Bassignana, a village a few miles away where the Tanaro merges into the River Po. The singer, though, had to face the Italian Fascist regime censorship and EIAR soon banned his American-styled songs.

The top song of World War II, however, was the nostalgic "*Lili Marlene*". Probably the most popular war-time song ever written, it began as a poem about a young German sentry on watch in World War One; set to music on the eve of the second world conflict, its popularity grew throughout the pubs and cabarets of Germany. Soldiers on both sides of the conflict soon carried the song over the continents. On the Axis side a famous voice singing Lili Marlene was that of the Swedish-born Zarah Leander, the leading female star of Nazi-Germany's film industry. The German-born screen icon Marlene Dietrich, a staunch anti-Nazi, performed for the Allied troops on different fronts and sang Lili Marlene whose starting English lyrics are:

> Underneath the lantern,
> By the barrack gate
> Darling I remember
> The way you used to wait
> T'was there that you whispered tenderly,
> That you loved me,
> You'd always be,
> My Lilli of the Lamp-light,
> My own Lilli Marlene

Radio dramas, or plays, were broadcast regularly as well. In those pre-television times they provided an internationally popular form of entertainment. Listeners could not see them, of course, so performances relied heavily on dialog, music and sound effects, to evoke the characters and action in each listener's imagination. Some programs were designed expressly for juniors, but there was nothing wrong in Luciano listening to most of the adult features, like light and amusing comedies - except when they lasted past his bed-time. Then a different, foreign, radio station operated in Italian, but it was officially illegal to listen to it, and could cost a fine and confiscation of the receiver. It was the BBC *Radio Londra* where the enemy news and propaganda could reach those who secretly dared to listen. The British colonel Harold Stevens (dubbed *Colonnello Buonasera*) provided polite, engaging talk, with plenty of news suggesting the military situation of the Axis armies had turned for the worse. Luciano was only allowed to listen to those broadcasts once; he never forgot its introductory theme tune, a sort of African drum-beat: "TUM, TUM, TUM...... TUM;..... TUM, TUM, TUM..... TUM". He also remembers some of the puzzling, apparently meaningless short phrases read by a different voice after the colonel's addresses: "The cow gives no milk", "The eagle flies". Those were coded messages directed to the partisans or Allies' special corps sent behind the lines to fight the Germans alongside the Italian Resistance.

The frightening noises of weaponry and explosions as well as the words and sounds coming out of that "magic box" called a radio, were obviously only part of the sound track of an ideal movie on Luciano's war years, though an essential one. Curiously a firearm shot and the story of that magic box have something to do with each other. One of the first critical experiments (on 8 December 1895) by Marquis Guglielmo Marconi, the Italian forerunner of radio communications, involved sending a signal from his villa near Bologna to a telegraphic device on the side of the hill opposite: his butler signalled "roger" - all OK - from there by firing a shotgun!

Pietra Marazzi as shown in a Nineteen-forties post card

The Montecastello's ferry in the Nineteen-thirties

*Tanaro River, 1943: Luciano and little sister
on Dad's skiff after visiting the ferry*

*Tanaro River, 1944: Luciano, cousin Gabriele,
little sister and Mom on the Montecastello's ferry*

Grandmother Giuseppina in the late nineteenth century

One of the RSI Postal Service's stamps Denouncing the militarily useless destruction of art threasures by the Alllies

A pre-WWII issue of the weekly devoted to junior Fascist youth

Bricco San Michele, 1945: Dad, Cini,
Luciano and Pasqualino on the pastures

Bricco San Michele, 1945: Cini, Luciano
and Mariuccia on a bread-baking day

The 1936 elite Fascist youth cruise to south America:
Luciano's Dad worried a lot for those kids!

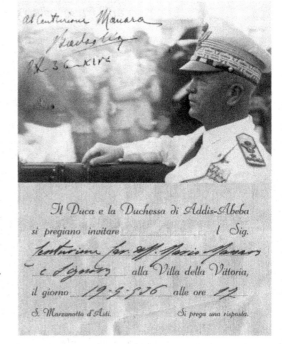

Marshall Badoglio's
1936 appointment to
Duke of Addis Ababa:
party invitation to
Luciano's parents

Winter 1942/43: Luciano's Dad as LUCE Institute's war correspondent on the eastern front

Don River's front, winter 1942/43: Italian troops retreating in a Mario Manara's photo

The pass issued to Mario Manara by his friend Davide; it reads:
Liberty Volunteers Corp Assault Brigade Garibaldi "Alessandria's Martyrs" Head office 1 —
Manara Mario is authorized to make his way through the area to reach this office so as to negotiate a solution to important issues
Ordered by the Chief of Staff Ulisse
2 October 44

13. Harder Times

Luciano's life at the village in the very first months of 1944 mostly carried on as usual: he honourably attended the third year of elementary school, played his much-loved games, hailed the awakening of the countryside after a really cold winter, read more books and barely felt any threat from the war. Yet some major events lurked to worry him and lose a lot of the confidence he had enjoyed till then: first came the bombing of Alessandria on Sunday April 30, Ascension Day.

In mid-morning the speechless boy, like most of the other villagers, had turned his head to stare up into the sky and couldn't bring himself to lower it again to look ahead, even when he was walking uphill: countless huge planes as never seen before were cruising at high altitude in a sort of slow carousel producing an unprecedented, deafening rumble. Eventually the deadly flock, of Boeing B-17 Flying Fortresses, faded westbound while strange tiny bright objects gently fluttered down all over the place, adding a surreal touch to the already confusing scene. Nobody there could imagine that those metalized paper strips – code-name Windows – were used to confuse the anti-aircraft radars, although there were none in Alessandria or, most probably, anywhere else in Italy. Then thunderous explosions started and those who had reached the top of the hill saw Alessandria burning; soon the dark clouds of smoke rising from the town next to the village could be seen anywhere from Pietra. The Alessandria paper *Il Piccolo* ("The Little One") on May 5 meticulously reported the carnage: "259 casualties of whom 45 youths and children, 17 servicemen, hundreds wounded". Its comments about the crews of the offending planes were: "....Pilots of mixed races of barbaric descent, recruited by the Americans to convey their hatred and aversion to the secular European civilization....". During World War II,

Alessandria was a tactical military target subjected to frequent Allied bombing until the very last days of the German occupation. On 5 April 1945, 160 died, including 60 children from a nuns' nursery school. That was possibly the last of a long series of Allied air raids on northern Italy consisting of low-altitude bombing and attacks by small formations (three aircraft) of B29 Martin Marauder medium twin-engine bombers. In the March 1945 issue of the National Geographic Magazine's article by Lt. B.C. McCartney USAAF, the caption to a dramatic aerial view of town, including the star-shaped Citadel reads: "Masonry explodes like a volcano; Alessandria loses a highway bridge… what a beautiful target, American bombers exclaimed as they regretfully passed by…". How different the ones cruising at two thousand feet felt from those laboring on the ground!

The capture of Rome by the Allies on 5 June 1944, achieved only after one year of furious battles following the invasion of Sicily, was mostly greeted by the residents, especially since the Germans evacuated the town, without attempting any resistance. Rome, in fact, had been declared an "open city" and was thus spared many casualties and much ruin. Earlier in March, however, some partisans, regardless of that and of Kesselring's policy of retaliation on civilians for losses of his men while away from the front line, hid a bomb in a trash can and it killed more than thirty Germans in a police squad marching through town; the appalling toll for that militarily useless action was the merciless slaughter of over 300 hostages in the *Fosse Ardeatine*.

With the Allies' arrival the worst was over for the Romans, but those living further north like Luciano felt increasingly uncomfortable as the actual conflict drew closer. In the previous twelve months war had raged throughout southern Italy. Whereas the Axis legions scarcely defended Sicily after the Allies' sea-born invasion of July 1943, the attack on the Italian mainland by British and U.S. troops was strongly opposed by the Germans and their loyal Italian corps. Early in September that year the British crossed the Strait of Messina (on the 3rd) moving on to Calabria, the "toe" of the boot-shaped Italian peninsula. The mixed U.S.-British forces landed on the "shin" (on the 9th) in Salerno, just south of Naples, where they met strong German resistance; the Allies entered Naples only on October 1st. More Allied troops landed on the '"heel" in early September and captured the ports of Taranto and Brindisi and the cities of Bari and Foggia, the former, like Brindisi, on the Adriatic Sea. It was because of these more successful Allied landings on the "heel", which threatened the

Germans at their rear, that they eventually decided not to defend Naples. The Axis forces of General Albert Kesselring including about 15 German divisions, after temporarily checking the Allies advance north of Naples, were positioned on a system of heavily fortified defence lines (known as the Gustav line) running 100 miles from the Tyrrhenian Sea at the mouth of the River Garigliano through Cassino and over the Apennine Mountains, to the Adriatic coast where the River Sangro flows out. Thus the Allies' northward advance was blocked and it took them till late May 1944 to fight their way through. They had also bypassed the Gustav line by landing seaborne troops at Anzio, some 30 miles south of Rome, on January 22, but once again, meeting strong resistance from the Germans (supported by the newly-established Italian Special Marine Corps of Prince Valerio Borghese) they were repelled and could not move on to Rome for quite a while.

Luciano, almost nine and about to finish the third year of elementary school, obviously knew little of most of the wartime developments and only much later in life could he read enough of that tragic story to gain an insight on how and why the world turned out so cruel. However, his interest in knowing more, and his apprehension, were well established when he learnt that the enemy had taken Rome. He learned too that on their tough route there, the invaders had paid a high price in several merciless battles around Montecassino, where a precious historic monument, an abbey founded by St. Benedict of Nursia in the 6th century, was destroyed in a series of heavy Allied air-raids that had been ordered in the mistaken belief it was a German stronghold. Besides the magnificent old building atop of a rocky hill overlooking the town of Cassino, the Abbey's archives containing hundreds of ancient historical documents and rare manuscript codices were irreplaceably lost. (the abbey was rebuilt after the war). In the monastery, the bombing only killed Italian civilians seeking refuge there and no dead German troops were found there. Yet most bombs fell elsewhere and killed German and Allied troops alike. In the days that followed German paratroopers took up positions in the ruins which provided better protection from air and artillery attacks; thus from a purely military viewpoint the bombing of Montecassino was counterproductive for the Allies. Documents showing that in December 1943 Field Marshall Albert Kesselring had given the order to exclude the abbey from the German defensive lines, while informing the Vatican and the Allies accordingly, add to the latter's blame for deliberately destroying it.

Many more treasures of Italian art were damaged or destroyed in World War II and the postal service of the *Repubblica Sociale Italiana* (RSI), the "new" Fascist nation of northern Italy established by Mussolini in October 1943, issued a series of stamps each showing one of those damaged monuments with the Latin comment: *Hostium rabies deruit* (Destroyed by the enemy's rage). That was how Luciano learned about the Montecassino abbey's tragic fate.

As the war took a series of unfavorable turns for his motherland, Luciano worried increasingly, feeling threatened as if by a barbarian invasion. Indeed the "barbarians", he reasoned, were once more in Rome, although this time arriving from the south, rather than crossing the Alps. Yet he also knew that on June 6, the day after Rome was seized, the Allies had started the invasion of northern France with their landing in Normandy, one of the most spectacular and bloody operations of World War II: D-Day. As he became aware of these developments, if only summarily, Luciano started to wonder whether there was any hope that the Axis forces could reverse the menacing trend of the conflict. The Fascist radio's propaganda that the boy listened to, made him realize that Germany had been working secretly to develop unprecedentedly powerful weapons capable of reaching far-off targets. He was, in fact, quite excited when a few days after the Allies seized Rome, the news spread that the first of these weapons had hit London. That was the V1, a sort of unmanned, small jet plane powered by a rocket engine and loaded with explosive. Thousands more were launched on southeast England causing almost ten thousand casualties, mostly civilians. Then, in September, came the V2, the world's first ballistic missile - the forerunner of all modern rockets, both weapons and spacecraft. The Germans sent out those deadly instruments as retaliation for the Allies' "terror bombing" which had devastated their cities since 1942.
Interestingly, the Americans and Russians all hastily schemed how to get hold of as many German scientists and engineers as possible who had been involved in the secret weapons program. Shortly after the end of the war, quite a few of those men with their families and belongings (including domestic animals!) were displaced to Russia on a specially scheduled train; some settled there permanently. The Americans got Werner von Braun, the central figure in Germany's rocket development program, and took him and some of his team to the U.S. as part of a secret operation; he covered a key role in the American Space Agency's endeavors leading to them putting the first man on the Moon in July 1969.

The V1 and V2 were only part of the non-conventional weapons Nazi Germany was working at. In the fall of 1944 a young Italian journalist sent by Mussolini, Luigi Romersa, who became a lifelong friend of von Braun, was admitted into the secret base at Peenemunde on the Baltic Sea where he could learn about - and report to the Duce - the other projects in progress there. Romersa's book "*Le Armi Segrete di Hitler*", (Hitler's secret weapons) - published in the third millennium, adds to the notion that the Nazis struggled hard to obtain what would certainly have changed the course of the war, if not of history: a nuclear weapon. Fascist Italy meanwhile had successfully pioneered unconventional warfare techniques at sea. All that Luciano knew at the time was only the report of some bold Italian Navy frogmen who had sunk or damaged several Allied ships moored in Mediterranean ports, using time bombs attached to their targets with magnets. Only later in life did he learn that, besides human daring, a good deal of unprecedented technology plus training and planning had been essential for accomplishing those missions, admired even by their foes. The new secret Italian weapons were small underwater assault vehicles, nicknamed *maiali* (pigs); each consisted of a torpedo ridden by a crew of two who breathed oxygen from the first rebreather fitted with sophisticated technical solutions. Although specially adapted submarines carried the pig - supposed to blow up with its target - as close as possible to it, the crew was left to its own devices once the mission was accomplished. However, these were not meant to be suicidal attempts and many of the brave frogmen survived. The leader of these covert nighttime operations (described in his 1953 book "*Sea Devils*", ISBN 1-55750-072-X) was the Roman prince and submarine commander Junio Valerio Borghese, awarded the Gold Medal of Military Valor, the highest Italian military decoration; his plans included a spectacular human torpedo attack on New York City, which almost materialized, if it had not been for the 1943 armistice.

Several of Borghese's men were also awarded the Gold Medal: one, Luigi Ferraro, engaged in sport and recreational underwater activities after the war as an organizer, inventor and producer of innovative diving gear. Luciano, as a keen SCUBA diver and amateur underwater photographer in his adult life, became familiar with Ferraro's company, Technisub, which was later merged into a multinational group. The boy also happened to know of the unconventional aerial warfare in the Pacific: in October 1944, as the Americans threatened the Japan's home islands, specially trained *Kamikaze* pilots started voluntarily to crash their aircrafts laden with explosives into enemy ships.

Different, undesirable developments in 1944 made Luciano's existence much less enjoyable, besides his greater awareness of the almost-world-wide hostilities which were moving closer and making things worse for his home country. One was the other "domestic war", the fratricidal conflict between Italians who remained loyal to Mussolini and his German allies, and those who either joined the Allies fighting Hitler's armies in the south of the country, or engaged in sabotage and secret operations in Northern Italy, where the new Fascist state RSI had been established; the northerners were the partisans fighting in the Resistance. In the beginning (September 1943 Armistice) most partisans were simply part of the disbanding Italian Royal Army who decided to hide out in the wild. Soon, however, the anti-Fascist political parties revived after Mussolini was deposed on July 25th, inspired several different military-like organized groups. Eventually a Committee of National Liberation (CNL) was established to take control of them in agreement with the Allies. Relations between the different groups were not always good and occasionally they fought each other. In addition the Allied secret services meddled, with divisive intents, typically the American OSS (the precursor of CIA which followed in 1947), who disliked the filo-Soviet units.

Luciano realized that the partisans, namely those belonging to the Communist Garibaldi Brigades operating in the nearby Asti province, posed a threat to his father Mario's life. Renato Ricci, who shortly before Luciano's birth had appointed Mario President of the Asti section of the foundation for youth welfare and patriotic education ONB, was one of Mussolini's top men, siding with him after the turnabout of summer 1943. Later on, shortly after the RSI was proclaimed, he took command of its first established armed forces, the GNR, mostly engaged in police duties and in fighting the partisans. The GNR was made up of the former Fascist Militia plus volunteers and the Carabinieri, the King's police (the latter were soon interned in Germany).

Rodolfo Graziani, a former commander-in-chief of the Royal Army, attempted set up non-politicized RSI armed forces: Italian youth were drafted and volunteers from disbanding army units were sent to Germany for training. Four disciplined, motivated divisions returned to Italy but, contrary to the original plans, they were deployed, often ill-armed, primarily in anti-partisan operations behind the front line, rather than against the Allies; the population as well as the German combatants disliked them. The most hated, though, were the often cruel armed Fascist volunteer groups known as Black Brigades, many of them flawed by indiscipline, disarray, lack of training and the presence of criminals released from jail. Some joined the Brigades for personal, opportunistic reasons, but there were also quite a few Fascist-educated youths with genuine patriotic sentiments.

Those were hand-to-mouth times and it was no surprise if a Black Brigade raided homes in the countryside for food, betraying its police duties (but so did the partisans). It was much worse when they set fire to the houses of people purportedly hiding or helping partisans (who in turn retaliated by punishing alleged informers the same way). On both sides there was room for heroic conduct inspired by opposing sincere credos and for private crimes which had nothing to do with the clashing beliefs that led to a raging civil war whose divisive heritage has still not been completely extinguished in the third millennium. Sadly almost seven decades after the end of the war, some Italian public figures still denied shamefully that those who died "for the wrong idea" deserved to be mourned just as much as their opponents. No wonder that during the conflict the population at large, rather than siding openly with the partisans or, even less, backing those who fought them, was mostly scared and maintained a wait-and-see mode, settling in a "grey zone" as the late Enzo De Felice wrote. Much like the nineteenth-century *Risorgimento*, whether the Italian Resistance was a popular revolution is only an interpretation stretched out by those interested in fostering its myth.

The armed corps of the RSI further included the Financial Guard (special corps dealing with financial crime and smuggling) and the "private army" of Prince Borghese, the revived *Decima Flottiglia MAS* (X^a MAS ,10th Assault Vehicle Flotilla, or *Decima MAS*) formerly engaged in the glorious secret sabotage operations at sea. In September 1943 Borghese signed a treaty of alliance with the Germans; his men fought in land campaigns alongside them as a fully independent anti-partisan force comprising up to 18,000 members. The Borghese's men also earned a good combat reputation fighting on the frontline against the Allies at Anzio and on the Gothic Line. In the last months of the war, X^a MAS units were dispatched to the eastern Italian border against Tito' s Yugoslav partisans who were trying to annex Istria and Venezia Giulia. Like the partisans, though, profound internal divisions plagued those who fought under Mussolini and their relations with the RSI civil authorities were seldom good.

Ricci reinstated Luciano's father in Asti, but regrettably not to resume his once popular job in the Opera Balilla. Mario's comeback had a lot to do with the GNR. He was not responsible for it, nor did he take part in its operations but, as one of Ricci's more trustworthy associates, was in charge of administration and logistics. That of course made no difference to most of the partisans - except one of them, Davide Lajolo, nicknamed Ulisse as a commander of the Garibaldi Brigades. Mario commuted almost daily between Asti and Pietra Marazzi on a huge military version of a Guzzi *Alce* (meaning elk) motorbike, like the one he had used to visit his family in the Dolomites while in Belluno (a similar model is visible in his photo of a Russian prisoner on the Don frontline). Luciano, formerly proud of his father's motorcycle, worried as he learned he travelled in an area subject to partisan operations. Mario had been given a pass by his friend Davide, but that was hardly meant to provide full protection: as a rule of thumb for survival in those wild times many, depending on the circumstance, probably thought it wiser to shoot the suspect before searching his pockets! At some time (early in 1944 ?), Davide showed up in Pietra Marazzi. Luciano enjoyed seeing him again and the visitor was also pleased to see how grown up his little friend he had first met in Ancona had become. Yet something odd went on between Luciano's Dad and Davide during that visit, although the boy only sensed it vaguely and the most he remembered was feeling sort-of scared despite being reassured with a hug by both men at the same time. That was probably when Davide was urging Mario to give up his job in Asti, which he kept until the very last days of the war. Decades later Luciano heard two contrasting versions of the same episode, which occurred some time after Davide's visit: a GNR armory in Asti had been seized by partisans in one of the Garibaldi Brigades. Davide always maintained that Mario knew about it and had provided the keys to the place where the arms were stored. However, Luciano's Dad never admitted he had helped, blaming the whole thing on some "dirty trick" by Davide who had asked him for shelter.

No partisans' action was ever seen around Pietra Marazzi, although in the last days of April 1945, when it became clear that the Germans had gone, all sorts of motor vehicles, most carrying people in arms, waving red flags, started to cruise along the road around the village, passing in front of Luciano's house; some villagers who by no means had taken the winners' side before, joined in hailing the motorized crowd.
However, in fall 1944 a search was made, jointly by German and GNR troops; the operation was mainly intended to catch young men subject to military draft who had gone into hiding rather than registering. As a matter of fact one of these, Danilo Cecchetti, an eighteen-year-old

from Pietra, had spent the winters of 1943 and 1944 in a small hut in the middle of a vineyard, and his younger sister Maria would occasionally sneak in bringing some food. Luciano was first woken up at dawn when grandmother Giuseppina passed by his bed with Beppe Ponzano, cousin Gabriele's older half-brother, and showed him how to climb up into the attic through a narrow, woodworm-eaten, wooden staircase whose only door opened in that very bedroom. The boy hardly realized what was going on though he very soon got the picture, when grandmother returned with a "gigantic" German serviceman. She showed the staircase to the apparently embarrassed, "softly-treading" visitor (Luciano's little sister, who remained asleep, was in that room too), but cautioned him that some of the steps might give way if overloaded. So Beppe escaped capture.

Some time after that search, a Black Brigade pickup came to Pietra in daytime. The crew was only looking for food and Luciano's grandpa Joe had just slaughtered his pig. According to an eye witness, cousin Gabriele, then living with Joe, that Brigade's visit turned out to be a sort of comics: in no way intimidated by the juniors who claimed his pork products were being hoarded illegally, he kept yelling all the time that those thieves should have earned their good luck by first helping him with the hard work in the fields. Meanwhile the driver, an overweight, middle-aged, bald guy, was complaining to Joe's wife Teresa that he hadn't had a decent meal in ages - reportedly while gratefully enjoying a dish of tasty soup she had fixed that day!

The next Black Brigades' raid around the end of that year was quite different: a tragic one. Regardless of the long-standing curfew, some villagers used to meet here and there after dinner to play cards; they would later disband in silence and sneak back home. One night, however, just when they had got outside a house into main street and said goodnight to each other, the high beams of a Black Brigade motor vehicle caught the party: one fugitive was shot dead; the next morning Maria Fongi Boccone, his eldest daughter, did not join Luciano at school

14. Things aren't any better, but...

When the Allies eventually seized Rome in June 1944, Luciano worried they could soon reach the Po valley and his own whereabouts in the north; but he was wrong - it took them till the following spring to get there. The German forces retreated gradually to a first line of resistance crossing Florence, thus completing another excellent chain of defence further north. It ran from the Tyrrhenian Sea, midway between Pisa and La Spezia, to the Adriatic between Pesaro and Rimini, through the natural defensive wall of the Apennines. It was dubbed "The Gothic Line" and included concrete-reinforced artillery pits and trenches, anti-tank ditches, machine-gun and mortar positions. After several furious offensives by the Allies in September and some of the hardest battles of the Italian campaign, there was no final breakthrough before the autumn rains. Then winter made Kesselring's troops' resolute opposition insurmountable (reinforced by effectives from one of the German-trained Italian divisions, the Monterosa Alpine Corps). Meanwhile, behind the Axis front lines there was intense disruptive partisan activity, with ambushes and sabotage. This may have been lucky for the Allies, but it meant additional suffering for the population, which was subject to some of the cruellest-ever German retaliation, fatal to hundreds of innocent civilians.

Luciano's worries, however, were shifting from the Allies' eventual conquest of northern Italy, to the already distressing threat to his father from the partisans, which could only get worse once the war ended. In addition, the boy's mood tended to be gloomy for several other reasons. At school, for instance, when he enrolled in fourth grade in September 1944, things were quite different. The finger-wagging, bespectacled Mr. Ventrini, a severe, old-fashioned teacher, was not in the least impressed by Luciano's fluent conversation on a variety of subjects and his imaginative writings, which had earned him success in third grade. The hard-nosed, elderly new teacher cared a lot more about discipline (and maths!) than the previous one, the lovely congenial Miss Baldi. The boy no longer enjoyed school, which from then on meant only duty rather than fun. He also lost a lot of self-confidence among his peers, not least because of a strange homemade sleeveless winter jerkin, supposed to replace his coat which no longer fitted, that he wore reluctantly. It was a sort of poncho, a kind of Andean "cloak" made of a square of woolly fabric with a hole in the middle that you put your head through. His mother had cut down her husband's military cape and dyed it dark blue; she also fitted it with a home-cured rabbit fur collar. Wrapped in this mantle Luciano, who might have looked cute to an adult, felt sadly abashed - a fish out of water among his peers! He never complained at home, though, because he realized his parents couldn't afford anything better!

Another disappointment arose with the boy's hated struggle to learn how to play a musical instrument. First of all, the previous year aunt Tina had insisted he should take lessons from her patient friend Enrica, a professional pianist. However, his attempts were most frustrating – his fingers behaved as if they were frozen on the keyboard and he could not do even the simplest exercises! After that Luciano's Dad thought his son might do better with the accordion; during the war he had met a Russian boy who was a great success with that instrument and was applauded enthusiastically by the Italian troops. The Allies were coming soon, so might Luciano too be better off with them if he could offer some musical talent? So we see the unenthusiastic but dutiful boy commuting twice a week on his bike between home and a place a few miles away where an old trumpet player lived. That involved pedalling up and down along the unpaved, bumpy road over a hill midway along the route, wearing his instrument like a backpack. The trip was safe enough as far as (absent) motor traffic, but the downhill slopes posed a threat and Dad warned Luciano to be careful. Still, how could he resist for long from taking advantage of Newton's gravitation law to feel some of the joy of speeding downhill, until… a deep scar on his left knee reminded him lifelong of his father's warnings!
The old musician only taught Luciano how to read music but his pupil didn't really care, let alone learn; he preferred to try and play by ear. That worked out only to some extent as far as the instrument's right-hand manual keys were concerned - used for playing the melody, like a piano keyboard; it helped that the boy could at least see which keys

he was supposed to press. However, the buttons on the left-hand side were not visible to the person playing the accordion so he never made much progress with the accompaniment those buttons were meant to produce. Thus, even when Luciano managed to play a recognizable melody – although never without a few glitches ! – it didn't have much flavor, like a sort of salad with no dressing!

Disturbing emotions were aroused when Luciano made two trips to nearby Alessandria, once when he was taken there for fun by Dad and the other when Mom went to town with Dad to an opera. Earlier in April Alessandria had suffered a first spectacular, massive, devastating air raid, whose smoke Luciano had seen from the village's southwest hill; then occasionally more bombing followed, some by single fighter bombers aiming for the bridges and causing only circumscribed damage. It may seem strange therefore that people would leave their safe shelter in the countryside, and take a risk by going to town just for pleasure. The second world conflict was not fought only in the front lines, as tragically illustrated by the appalling number of civilian casualties, exceeding that of combatants in most countries. Yet the hearts of towns continued to beat under the bombs. During its almost three-year siege, Leningrad (now St. Petersburg) lived on despite air raids and famine: theaters, libraries and museums remained open, students continued their studies and passed their exams, Dmitri Shostakovich wrote his Seventh Symphony, *Leningrad*, and it was performed.
Luciano and his Dad's bike trip to Alessandria went smoothly on the way there; the boy was puzzled rather than scared by the ruin he saw. Streets were mostly free from rubble but some inner walls of bombed apartment buildings stood, showing the interiors with pictures and fabrics still hung there: the boy thought they looked like dolls' houses. There weren't many people around: the place looked sleepy. While approaching the town center, however, Luciano heard some not so far-off, distinct, sharp noises repeated every few seconds: were they shots? He looked at Dad and frowned. Mario reassured him with a smile and a few minutes later they reached the town's main square where tournaments were held, and found some youths practicing *tamburello*. This is a game played on a court about a hundred yards long and half as wide, with rules and scoring like tennis; the ball is a bit heavier than a tennis ball, and is batted around with a hand gadget, known as the *tamburello*, made of a round wooden frame with a cow-hide cover tightly stretched over it; it is like a tamburine. Luciano knew there was a couple of those in his ancestors' home, but

had never seen anybody playing with them. The game had been imported to Piedmont in centuries past from bordering France, whence the northwest Italian region borrowed quite a few customs and idioms; a foregoer is mentioned in Julius Caesar's commentaries on the wars he fought in Gaul.

On the return trip the pair soon crossed again the out-of-town bridge over the Tanaro and took a right turn onto the less than half a mile of gently sloping paved road, before getting to the intersection from which the rest of their route home was bumpy, along a road strewn with pebbles and potholes. At a certain point they came across a few people and a town policeman standing around an uncovered corpse lying in a small pond of reddish-brown blood: that was no road accident. When Mario spotted the scene, it was too late to stop his son, make a U-turn and take a distant roundabout route, no matter how long it would have taken them. Actually the boy swiftly overtook his father and found himself faced with what he shouldn't have seen only at the last moment when a few yards away, and barely stopped in time not to bump into a bystander. He stood stunned, still clumsily astride his bike and, as soon as his disappointed Dad picked him up, he closed his eyes and vomited. The boy's physical distress was short-lasting and the bike ride back home was otherwise undisturbed. He remained speechless, though, all the way and even at home he still wouldn't say a word, but sipped a little hot milk and was taken to bed. At least one of his parents had to sit by until he fell asleep: it took an unusually long time.

Neither the next day nor later on, the boy never mentioned that scary experience, but its clear-cut view persisted, indefinitely stamped in his mind, where it imprinted the full notion of what a bloody killing meant and looked like - so terribly different from the innocent war games he had played with his little pal Enzo in Belluno! From then on, each time Luciano went back mentally to the tragic events of those times whose stories he had been told, this insight served to illustrate all the evil he had hardly been aware of at all. His fears for the future too followed a similar pattern, in the first place for his Dad's life, because he commuted through areas where partisans were active; and sometimes the boy's already gloomy outlook worsened worryingly into anxiety. No wonder he felt the same when his parents went to town for the opera show – and it got even worse later on.

Although he had never mentioned it to anybody, Luciano was already suffering occasional bouts of anxiety at bed-time: They dated from those frightening nightly air raids blamed on the elusive *Pippo* and caused a sort of paracusia as specialists call it, i.e. hearing voices that seem real and yet aren't. He perceived the sounds rising up from downstairs as deafening and threatening. Thank God that didn't last long but, after his parents' trip for the opera (Mom also got her hair done), Luciano developed the phobic idea that his mother had gone away and somebody else was pretending to be her. Again the boy didn't tell anybody, but for a while he kept asking Mom curious questions about past events that only the real Mom could have answered. Similar psychological breakdowns, displayed differently or sometimes not at all, must have been common among people of any age more or less exposed to the strains of wartime events, but possibly the youngest ones, like Luciano, were the least susceptible to permanent, disabling fear and anxiety.

Beside air raids and the partisans' guerrilla operations against fascist and German regular forces in large parts of northern Italy, an additional serious concern for the population were bandits. Unlike the generally solitary murderous robbers of the first decades of the XXth century who were accountable for holdups, banditry in the last years of World War II mainly involved burglaries by merciless gangs, aiming at remote and isolated dwellings. They were feared by village dwellers too, no matter that they were unlikely to target communities. Thus in Pietra Luciano learned what that rod leaning by the door was for: at night locking the doors was not safe enough, one had better bar them too!

The best-known gang active in lower Piedmont as well as in Liguria was led by a German Navy deserter, a Czech called Thomas Hozak, who was caught and executed (or killed by a rival gang?) shortly after the war. In May 1944 a horrendous crime was committed in a nearby village - only a few miles southwest of Alessandria - that was much discussed in Pietra too and remembered as the *Borgoratto* ("ratville") massacre. Two families and some of their guests were slaughtered; an eighteen-month-old baby hidden under the blankets in bed was the only one spared. The sole indisputable record of that event is in the *Borgoratto* town registry where there are thirteen names of people who died on 17 May 1944, all "at about one o clock". They include a boy aged eight and a ten-year-old girl.

Besides a couple of short news items in Alessandrias's weekly *Il Piccolo* (one announcing the carnage, the other the execution of the purported culprits), several partly contrasting written accounts of the event, based on non-eyewitnesses' information, appeared only long after the end of the war. Only a few aspects, though, seem fairly agreed and more or less credit-worthy. The scene was two houses in the country far outside the township, on the left of the River Bormida and several hundred yards from each other. The Buzzis and their guests were the gang's target, in all probability not because of their work as modest land owners and vegetable growers, which just masked their thriving black market trade - there were too many outsiders visiting them to go unnoticed in the village. The Cellerinos, their neighbors, were most likely only unwitting and unwelcome witnesses to the gang - in the wrong place at the wrong time! On July 27 three former Italian soldiers, from an army unit disbanded in September 1943, all from Sicily, were brought to Borgoratto and executed there by a Black Brigades squad; the villagers doubted they were the real culprits. They were buried in the village cemetery not far from the victims of the May onslaught. The precise reasons for that killing remained unfathomable.

Glimpses of sunlight breaking through may sometimes lighten the dark skies like those looming over Luciano's uneasy existence in 1944. A baby girl was born next door in late August. Luciano was not yet mature enough to sense the reassuring feelings of the adults there: no matter how hard the times, that new life meant confidence in a better future wasn't all lost. However, Luciano really enjoyed the baptism party a few weeks later. The newcomer was Carlo's second daughter, the young obstetrician who rented part of great-aunt Francesca's house across the fence as a home that was safer than town for his family during the war. Carlo of course loved his first-born Paola; his fondness for Luciano, though, may have been partly because he was a boy. Possibly the doctor had hoped his second-born would be a male – did he perhaps feel that society offered women only a subordinate role? (In Italy they voted for the first time in 1946). Yet Anna-Maria grew up to become a forerunner of the most evolved Italian feminine condition in the second half of the XXth century. As a student she travelled the world, including Muslim countries, became a successful architect, married and rewarded her dad with a boy grandchild!
When the bell tolled everybody, including Luciano, walked up to the church for the baptism. The ceremony lasted quite a while, following an ancient rite going back to the very beginning of organized Christian worship. After several prayers the priest turned to the two sponsors holding the baby by the baptismal font and asked them three times: "Dost thou Anna-Maria renounce Satan and all his works, the vain

116

pomp and glory of the world?" and each time he asked one of the sponsors replied: "I do renounce him". Then the vicar poured water from the font over the sleeping baby's head and she started bawling at the top of her voice! Luciano thought it was very funny. As people were slowly leaving the church, he stayed with his mother who wanted to say hello to Don Cesare. Mom had known him since the late 1920s when she was learning embroidery at the Saint Vincent Paul's Sisters house in Alessandria and had made several tablecloths for the village church's altars. Ten years before that baptism the priest had married Luciano's parents and the boy visited him occasionally to borrow books: probably one of them was Jules Verne's Twenty Thousand Leagues Under the Sea. When Luciano met him, Don Cesare Moretti was already a heavy old man, possibly suffering from diabetes, who moved ponderously, breathless with effort. Nonetheless he was devoted to his flock and walked around a lot to visit those who couldn't get to church or leave home and were otherwise in need; he was widely loved and respected in Pietra. Luciano realized only years later, when he found Don Moretti's book on the history of the village, that the humble man was in fact a scholar and fine writer. Reading it suggested the author had done plenty of digging into archives, for instance about the origin of the village's name. He had found that "Marazzi" was a family name, rather than deriving from "Maraci", the ancient Ligurian people described by Pliny as dwellers in lower Piedmont too. The old priest joined Luciano and Mom negotiating the steep stairs known as la scala santa (the holy steps) that led to Francesca Gillo's house where the party for Anna-Maria had been set up. The welcoming place had a big garden where the many guests tucked into a buffet that was unusually rich for those times - everything was home-made.

Francesca was not on good terms with her sister Giuseppina next door, Luciano's grandmother, and they actually never spoke to each other. With her husband, Valentino Gillo, a distinctive, good-looking man with a handlebar moustache - as he was depicted in a large portrait in the dining room - Francesca, then a widow, had spent several years in Holland, and souvenirs abounded all over the house. Quite impressive was the big oven built in the kitchen, but clad all over with the typical Dutch white tiles decorated in light blue with landscapes and windmills. Francesca had baked several pies for the occasion, which Luciano tasted eagerly, to her delight; she had never had children and loved Luciano's Dad and aunt Tina, and obviously the boy too: he saved lifelong great aunt's old big coffee mill decorated likewise the oven's tiles.

117

15. Nineteen-forty-five: the Showdown

In January 1945 the outlook was clearly bleak for the Axis forces. The previous year, when the Allies had swiftly invaded German occupied France after their landings in Normandy in June and in the French Riviera in August, Hitler, who had only just survived an attempt on his life in July, had hoped to overturn the outcome of the war on the western front with a winter counter-offensive in the Belgian Ardennes. Surprise and unfavorable weather for British and U.S. air support granted initial success to the Germans who, however, were compelled to withdraw by the end of December 1944, when they suffered devastating air bombing with substantial human and equipment losses; their chances of opposing the Allies' advance from then on were seriously compromised. Early in 1945 the western Allies, with a view to their final assault through the German line of resistance along the River Rhine, intensified their air raids including the militarily controversial ones on Dresden, between February 14 and April 17, causing the massacre of not less than twenty thousand people and destruction of the city center with its historic, cultural and art treasures. In late March the first Allied divisions breached the Rhine, meeting little opposition. German troops and civilians at that point mostly hoped that the British and American armies would sweep eastward promptly, reach Berlin and occupy as much of the country as possible before the Soviets passed the Oder Line. The Allies closed in as far as the River Elbe 60 miles from Berlin and on April 25 they were met there by the Red Army invading Germany at the end of its long advance through Eastern Europe.

On the eastern front, opened up by Hitler's armies' invasion of Russia in June 1941, the Soviets had been caught unprepared and disbanded. The Wehrmacht divisions, after advancing more than 400 miles, in mid-July were only 200 miles from Moscow and in December some of its vanguards entered the capital's outskirts. But the withdrawing Russians had destroyed anything that might be useful to the invaders, like railroads and bridges. The Red Army checked Germany's offensive in one of the coldest winters in history. The Germans' mechanized transport, tanks, artillery, aircraft and not always well-clad troops, stretched along a front almost 2000 miles long, were paralyzed: casualties added up to more than 700,000. Soviet counter-offensives had lasted throughout the winter of 1941-42 and the exhausted Germans tumbled back, though they still held most of their winter front. In the summer they launched an offensive in southern Russia, took the city of Rostov on the lower River Don and advanced further southward to the oil-fields of the Caucasus and north-eastward against Stalingrad on the Volga, an important industrial site producing armaments. The battle for the city, supported by devastating German bombing which turned most of it into ruins, lasted from August 1942 to February 1943; it was one of the bloodiest in history: civilian and military casualties totalled almost two million. Eventually the Germans who had not retreated were encircled in the city, with no possibilities of air supplies, and either surrendered or were annihilated. That was a first turning point in the war and, because of their heavy losses, the Germans never recovered their former aggressive potential.

Hitler's armies, however, after retreating from the Caucasus and from their advanced positions facing Moscow to straighter lines, started a counter-offensive in February 1943, which repelled the Soviets and re-established a front on the River Donets; later in July they engaged massively around the city of Kursk and thrusted deep into the Red Army's lines. It was the largest tank battle in history. The Germans' defeat cost them about 3000 tanks and 70,000 of the men who were driven back to the River Dnepr in Ukraine. From then on Germany's Russian campaign no longer posed any serious threat to the Soviet Union.

The invaders, far from turning about in a rout like Napoleon's in the previous century, were nonetheless forced for almost two years to keep up no more than resistance fighting to maintain an orderly, slow but constant retreat through eastern Europe. The last line of defence from the Red Army was set up in January 1945 on the River Oder, Germany's natural border with Poland. Bridgeheads were established early in March by the Russians who burst out in mid-April and by the 25th had encircled Berlin and linked up with the Allies on the Elbe. After Hitler's suicide on April 30, Admiral Donitz succeeded him and struggled to have most of his troops surrender to the British or Americans and not the Soviets, fearing the latter's vengeful reprisals: almost two million German soldiers escaped them. Meanwhile, early in 1945 four German divisions had been withdrawn from the Italian front to support the last defence of their motherland; the resulting untenable opposition to the Allied attacks by the residual Axis forces retreating into the Po valley caused them to surrender on April 29

In Luciano's circles, like elsewhere in northern Italy, information about how the war was progressing had always been scarce, imprecise and delayed; the official news insisted on the few momentarily successful operations of the Axis forces, like the V2 rocket launches on England or on the enemy's atrocities by massive air bombing of cities. On 20 October 1944 Milan was hit, and in its suburb Gorla, 184 little pupils, among others, perished with their teachers. Regardless of the propaganda intended to foster different opinions, early in 1945 everybody in northern Italy felt that the end of the fighting was likely to be a matter of weeks rather than months. Luciano's Dad had to make a trip to Milan, which worried the boy. Probably he had to report to his superiors about his job, but from then on he no longer commuted to and from Asti, to the boy's relief. One day in the spring Mario ferried his son and little daughter to a nicely blossoming woody area across the river; they looked for primroses to take home to Mom, but all of a sudden a German soldier appeared in front of them. The sturdy man was still clad with a winter uniform including an overcoat, sporting his helmet and a huge knapsack, and carried the typical Mauser shoulder weapon; oddly, he was alone. After exchanging a few words with Mario, while gently shaking his head, the newcomer crouched down to greet the little girl who clung to her Dad's legs. The two men talked a little more while Luciano had a long close look at the weapon and the soldier who eventually slowly walked away: he was aiming to get back to his far-off home, or at least that's what he hoped!

Luciano's permanent recollections of the last months of the war include two different upsetting episodes; both occurred shortly before that enjoyable trip across the Tanaro with his Dad and little sister; one was quite scary. The morning of the last Black Brigades raid on the village, the news spread that they were staying around. Luciano's mother had walked up to the bakery early and when he came out of school he decided to go and look for her there, just when she was returning home; they only missed each other because they chose different paths. As the boy moved out of the bakery after checking whether his Mom was there, several bursts of automatic rifle fire froze him at the door. This time he didn't panic like that night, about two years before, when his father had comforted him in bed, scared to death by *Pippo's* air raid. Knowing that the Brigades used to fire in the air from their vehicles, he had to figure out first which way they were coming, so as not to run into them. It could be either downhill on the upper road climbing to Montecastello, or from the road in the plain connecting Pietra to Alessandria; both roads led to the village main street and the bakery was midway. The advancing truck's creaking rather than the echoes of gunfire warned the boy the gang was approaching from below: in a moment they would appear on Luciano's right, at the turn where five years before, while playing at doing one of Mussolini's speeches on granddad Joe's home balcony, he had spotted his ox-drawn cart coming. He ran about a hundred yards to the left as fast as he could, where the main street turned left uphill; there was the steepest alley you could imagine and Luciano rushed down into it out of sight and got home. The bullets from a last burst of firing seemed to have just flown over his head, but how could the boy tell they actually went that close? From their sound, of course. Did they "hiss and whine and howl, and shriek and hum and whisper (or buzz)", like in the fiction writers' works who disappoint ballistics gurus? To hell with the sound: the bullets did fly over Luciano's head and he never liked anybody to argue that they didn't!

German troops hardly showed up in Luciano's village; a few operated a radio station in Montecastello's castle and lodged there. A few more had settled in Pavone (the name means peacock), the village on the River Tanaro side slope of the south-western hill facing Pietra; their quarters were in a palace, dubbed the castle, belonging to the Marquises of Bruno, an ancient Piedmont's family. The owners used to keep a couple of real peacocks in a spacious cage in their garden. Luciano had a chance to see the birds, but never heard anything about the German garrison until that gloomy day: ten men from Pietra had been abducted and were being detained in Pavone. There was plenty of reason to worry about the fate of those hostages. One of the German servicemen there had returned from leave without his weapon the night before and the captain wanted it back with the culprits within 24 hours. The hostages' families of course were desperate and the population at large feared the worst in view of the well-known vicious German reprisals elsewhere. Yet the whole tale was still a bit puzzling as there had never been any evidence of partisans in the area - and in any case they would have shot and killed the enemy. It was rumored that the German soldier must have got drunk with some locals (unlikely to have been from Pietra) and his buddies played that stupid, potentially deadly joke on him: it made a lot of sense, but was there any way out? Don Cesare Moretti thought there was and rushed up to Pavone - actually he took a long, slow walk, panting heavily - and met the captain. The priest offered in vain to stay himself in place of the hostages. However, by gaining the captain's confidence (who luckily was by no means a fanatic) he managed to negotiate, promised to regain the weapon and was given more time to do so. How Don Cesare got that weapon back is not known (some said a basket of onions had been found in the confessional - if so it couldn't have been missed!). However, he didn't manage right away and the agony of those directly involved seemed endless. Thank God (and Cesare Moretti). the hostages were eventually freed, which is what matters most. Otherwise there never was any credible information about the culprits (if any) or whether the German soldier had actually been boozy and forgotten the weapon. This episode, like the previous ones concerning his acquaintance with Don Cesare, left a permanent mark in Luciano's memory, encompassing admiration, devotion, confidence, respect, and more. Oddly enough, for quite a while after that (too long!) Luciano extended this deference to anyone wearing that noble man's habit, as if they automatically embodied the same dignity.

After Kesselring was switched to the more worrisome western front, Karl Wolff, a high-ranking SS officer, became the top German authority in (northern) Italy. Reportedly he had been secretly negotiating the surrender of his forces with the U.S. Office of Strategic Services in Switzerland, without informing either Hitler or Mussolini. In any case in the last weeks of April 1945, the unaware RSI combatants suddenly found themselves with no support from the surrendering Germans and could hardly oppose the Allies or check the partisans. Many tough fellows refused to surrender and continued to fight with a view to establishing a last line of resistance, as planned long before, in Valtellina, an alpine region north of Lake Como, where the River Adda forms a basin. One substantial event involved 6000 members of the Black Brigades dubbed "Column Pavolini" after their founder Vittorio Pavolini, one of Mussolini's henchmen and former minister of culture. However, fighting by the Fascists was mostly episodic; they soon lost control of most of the towns which, after the Germans had gone, were all easily taken over by the partisans by the end of April, and meanwhile the Allies arrived. Yet there were some unpredictable events worth telling, which most impressed Luciano when, as an adult, he learned about them from documents on those times.

Thus a Black Brigades unit in Romagna engaged a retreating German garrison to prevent their retaliations and destructions. Another episode involved an informal no-fighting pact between the commander of the RSI Alpine Corps division *Littorio*, Armando de Felice, and Augusto Adam, heading the partisans operating in the Aosta Valley, bordering France. This prevented an imminent invasion by the French pressing on the border with a view to annexing that territory, a move which eventually the Allies disapproved and thwarted.

As to the war's eventual developments in Luciano's area, Alessandria in the last days of April was the stage of a dramatic confrontation between the local partisans' representatives and the commanders of substantial German and RSI forces which had gathered there on the route of retreat, planning to continue into the Po valley. Reportedly the outcome was the only time the Germans surrendered (on the 29th) to the partisans rather than to the Allies, while American vanguards were entering town that very day.

Lieutenant General Kurt Jahn's IV Army Corps Lombardy, comprising General Farina's Marines San Marco division, had been deployed in defence of the western Ligurian littoral and Alpine border with France. They retreated in the last days of April, after negotiating a no-fighting agreement with the local CNL to transit through Alessandria province. Yet when they got close to the head town, the partisans, emboldened by learning that the Allies were getting closer, demanded their surrender. The German general's resolute refusal could have kindled a carnage involving the hapless population, but after endless, at times furious, talks he backed down, while Farina succeeded in subduing his hardliners, warding off civilian losses.

The last tragic wartime event in Pietra Marazzi occurred on April 25 when Pietro Quargnenti, known as Pidràs, was shot dead on his way back from working in the fields nearby Pavone. The German garrison, leaving its quarters there, was blamed for this last mindless, unforgivable crime.

Mussolini, disgruntled by the reportedly secret German capitulation, left his Government headquarters at Lake Garda and went to Milan on April 25, where Cardinal Schuster had been brokering an encounter with the top partisan representatives: it was not successful. That same evening he left the city for Como, followed

124

by his henchmen and some Fascist forces; the others disbanded locally. The Financial Guard unit there had already sided with the partisans and took as prisoners the Milan garrison of Prince Borghese's Decima flottiglia Mas, who decided to surrender without fighting.

Two days later Mussolini with his followers and long-time mistress Claretta Petacci, joined by a German anti-aircraft unit, left Como aiming northward along the western lakeside toward the Swiss border, but first met up with the partisans. A deal followed, with the Germans let go and the others held. Mussolini, his henchmen and Claretta were executed the next day near Lake Como and on April 29 their corpses were exhibited in Milan, at a gas station in a public square where several partisans had been put to death a year earlier. The dead Fascists were abused mercilessly at length by a large, hysterical crowd and eventually hung upside down on a frame.

Disparate versions of Mussolini's killing were given but most of the details of the events of those days remain obscure. Only speculation exists on the fate of important documents (including the purported correspondence with British Prime Minister Winston Churchill) which it was said that he always carried with him. Even the written reports (one kept private by the second pathologist was disclosed only years later) on the Duce's autopsy, done on April 30, are controversial. Years later Luciano, when at the University Medical school in Milan, read the official version by Professor Caio Mario Cattabeni, his teacher, who had struggled to do it "in a crowd of all sorts of people who normally shouldn't have been admitted" as he wrote. Whether Ms. Petacci's body was autopsied at all is not known.

In May 1945, the end of the long-endured suffering from a war that had hit civilians as never before was greeted in northern Italy with unconstrained exultation. The partisans, acclaimed by crowds, paraded in towns sporting their weapons; most wore red scarves because so many were bound to the Communist party, like the Garibaldi Brigades. Quite a few women marched as well, with similar pride. In a few days other shameful parades showed up, women with their heads shaved marching in front, urged on by mobs taunting and humiliating them; those reviled were or were presumed to have been Fascist or German collaborators. Often that was only the minor penance in broad daylight! Much worse happened mostly in the shade: "People's Tribunals" claiming to be courts were set up in a rush, and decreed summary executions. For several weeks, then for months - though gradually getting less intense - real terror reigned as thousands were slaughtered in northern Italy. Most of those whose life was taken, purportedly in retaliation, had had little or nothing to do with Fascism or the occupying Germans; and partisans deserve the blame for part of the carnage, with personal revenge, burglary or mobbing substantially behind it. Although a death toll of up to 300,000 was bandied about at the time, a reasonable figure worked out many years later with a historical approach, agreed by the different sides, was more like 10,000.

More civilian losses (possibly as many as 40,000), perpetrated by Yugoslav partisans, were reported in the hinterland of Trieste and Gorizia, the Karst region and south-west in Istria, which had been annexed to Italy after World War I. The slaughter was dubbed the *Foibe massacres*, after the deep Karst sinkholes (some several hundred feet) found in those regions, where many of the corpses were dumped; only a few were ever recovered. The first dreadful events started in September '43, with a swift invasion by the Yugoslavs while confusion reigned in the disbanding Italian armed forces left with no orders at the announcement, with no prior notice, of the armistice with the Allies. That continued till the end of the year when the Germans took back the area. Then, in April 1945, when the surrendering Germans retreated, the Yugoslav's invasion started again, with further killings. With such terror in the atmosphere, the majority of the Italians from Istria, Pola and Zara fled to other parts of Italy. Several historians believe the fate suffered by those people is an example of organized "ethnic cleansing". The dreadful event of the *Foibe* was long subject to a general cover-up, not least because of the persisting difficult relationships between Italy and Yugoslavia and the other countries bordering the region. Only in the last years of the 20th century was the long silence broken, with the publication of several books and historical studies. Eventually, in 2004, the Italian parliament passed a law establishing February 10 as the Day of Remembrance, in memory of the victims and the exodus.

16. The Aftermath

Spring 1945 saw exaltation among those finally released from the nightmare of the war, though it wasn't over for everybody yet. In the Pacific the conflict ended only in August with probably its fiercest episodes involving unprecedented arms of mass destruction: the atomic bombs on Hiroshima and Nagasaki. In places like northern Italy where a sort of civil war had been raging, the wake of the second world conflict was a time of *vae victis*, i.e. the bloody revenge of those playing the role of the winners against the Fascists and their sympathizers or presumed so. Luciano's family was in the losers' lot and paid its toll. Luckily enough, in their case it turned out to be nothing worse than threats, apprehension and distress, though the boy suffered some bullying.

There were no partisans' parades in the small village of Pietra Marazzi, but the usually sleepy road between Montecastello to the east and Pavone on the west, in front of the south side of grandmother Giuseppina's estate, suddenly became crowded with all sorts of motor vehicles going to and fro and honking their horns. People on cars and trucks, some sporting red shirts, often sang and waved red flags, or motorcyclists red scarves; that sort or carousel went on for several days. In a week or so came the Allies – a bit more discreetly: a unit of Brazilians, many of them black, apparently led by British officers, set up their quarters in Pavone where the Germans had stayed. They hardly ever swarmed into Pietra, which had never been known for its bright lights, but turned to Alessandria for fun. A bit later the Brazilians set up the Faà di Bruno Palace ballrooms for evening dancing where the locals were welcome. Once aunt Tina took Luciano to one of those venues. He enjoyed and never forgot the catchy melodies and, most of all, the surprising rhythm (samba) of *carioca* songs; this enthusiasm resurfaced much later on when, as a jazz fan, he hailed the world-wide successes of Bossa nova in the early Sixties.

Luciano's Dad, oddly enough, did not worry about the long-expected retaliation against the Fascists. It was imminent, as suggested by those jubilant Communist carousels along the road outside his home. Thus Mario had not planned on leaving the village for a safe shelter elsewhere and made a mistake because one morning some unfriendly people came looking for him. He escaped by a hair's-breadth from a window at the back of the house and ran uphill to Giuseppina's vineyard to hide in a huge cherry tree; there was no ladder, but Mario was one of the few in the village who could climb a tree without one, as he used to do.

Luciano, back from school, worried when he didn't see his Dad at lunch; some reassuring words from Mom didn't help much, since she herself seemed somehow "different". That afternoon he got really worried, like never before, even more so because he didn't want anybody to know: this was real anxiety! When at sunset Luciano spotted his father cautiously emerging from behind the straw bales stacked under the huge porch, he couldn't refrain from shouting: "Dad's back! Dad's back!". His father grabbed and hugged him, while gently pressing the palm of one hand against his son's mouth. Shortly afterwards Mario, in a touching face-to-face good-bye chat with his son, exhorted him to stay with grandmother and aunt Tina till school ended. He must have left right away and shortly after that mom should have left too, for a different destination. The next day, while her son was at school, unaware of events, Mother went to Alessandria to be questioned, as required by those who had missed Mario. They threatened that if she did not turn up they would set fire to the house. But dogs that bark seldom bite and the hapless woman got by unscathed. However, she didn't wait for further trouble, packed a few clothes and left, riding her bike, carrying her little daughter, Luciano's sister. It was no joke reaching Vinchio, about 30 miles away between the Monferrato and Langhe hills of Piedmont on bumpy, dusty roads, but the friendly springtime weather helped. There Nora was welcomed generously by her hostess Rosetta, Davide Lajolo's wife, whom she had first met in Ancona.

All that of course worried the unhappy Luciano a lot. Years before in his pre-school time he had spent a couple of months with grandmother Giuseppina without seeing his parents; then he had barely missed them. Now, much more grown-up, his enhanced understanding and awareness of the current untoward events made quite a difference. He only vaguely knew where his mother had gone; what about Dad after that close shave? For Luciano it was a difficult

128

time, especially because he wouldn't mention his preoccupation to anybody. Aunt Tina, however, must have instantly perceived her loved nephew's hidden gloom, partly because of her long experience with youngsters as a prep school teacher, and she kept both eyes on him!

At the time Tina was serving as a voluntary Red Cross nurse in Alessandria's military hospital; there she met a young captain of the "Cremona Combat Group" whose members, formerly part of the Italian Royal Army's "Cremona" division, had sided with the Allies and in the last months of the war they had clashed successfully with the Germans around Venice. The poor man had both legs crushed by a tank, and was admitted in critical conditions with gangrene, which he "miraculously" overcame thanks to a "miraculous" drug. So Luciano learned of penicillin, the first antibiotic. During World War II it sharply reduced the number of deaths and amputations due to infected wounds among Allied forces, saving an estimated 20% of lives.

The drug's story dates from long before. In 1928 Alexander Fleming in London had serendipitously discovered the antibacterial properties of the mould *Penicillium rubens*. From there to obtaining the actual drug, it took a considerable effort by him and others. The U.S. War Production Board planned the mass distribution of penicillin to the Allied troops fighting in Europe in July 1943 and it was in 1945, a few months after the drug had saved the Italian captain's life in Alessandria, that Dr. Fleming shared the Nobel Prize in Physiology or Medicine with E.B.Chain and H.W.Florey.

Aunt Tina's acquaintance with the wounded captain turned out to Luciano's favor, not only by learning about that breakthrough in the science of pharmacology - then in its infancy: he was destined to be deeply involved in that discipline throughout his adult life. The ailing captain read a lot, including American comic books the boy had never seen before; when aunt Tina brought him some the captain had discarded, Luciano eagerly plunged into that unprecedented, fascinating, reading experience. He had enjoyed adventures in novels like those by Emilio Salgari, but the comics, with their fascinating drawings and little speech balloons, left much less to the imagination and carried him away faster into their fantastic realms, rich in action. Two unforgettable main characters struck Luciano most, both by the same world-renowned American artist Lee Falk: "Mandrake the Magician" and "The Phantom". Mandrake, always attired for the stage, in formal white tie and tails, with a top hat, pencil-line moustache and scarlet-lined cape, fights all sort of evil-doers thanks to his unbeatable powers of hypnotism and illusion. As an example, the magician hero could throw his foe completely off course by putting a gigantic, menacing rat in front of him! The African Lothar, Mandrake's evil fighting companion, "the strongest man in the world", appears in short pants and a leopard skin, wearing a fez.

The Phantom, dubbed in Italian *L'Uomo Mascherato* (the masked man) sports a skin-tight red costume and a black mask; he has no supernatural powers but defeats his enemies thanks to superior strength and intelligence; in addition, he is an immortal ghost. Like Mandrake, the Phantom too battles against evil, inspiring moral sentiments.

 When Luciano took along one of his comic books and showed it to his school pals, not surprisingly their excitement didn't go unnoticed to the teacher. Mr. Ventrini grumbled; after a quick look at the book, criticized as bad reading, he cautioned Luciano against bringing anything of that kind to school again. Of course the teacher's judgment could only arouse the boys' curiosity and the whole class (in fourth grade boys and girl went to separate classes) asked to borrow the book from its owner. However, something upsetting happened when he was leaving school which prevented him lending it.

 Back home Luciano barely ate anything of the lunch laid on by grandmother; he had a long story of lack of appetite which sweet mom had been fighting consciously all the time. The boy's mood had hardly mattered, except on that hazy day which suddenly turned troublesome upon leaving school. He went outside pondering, walked to the porch and further on to the field. Corn had been sown that year and the rows of shoots, just sprouting, cut though the brown soil. Luciano moved along the edges, careful not to step on them. It seemed about to rain: the sturdy dark-brown mulberry trees surrounding the field had been pruned fiercely as usual and looked awkwardly "bald", each with three or four rounded stumps at the top of the trunk. The strips of grass between the trees looked dusky. Unlike the oaks growing naturally alongside the hilly roads, mulberry trees in the plains were planted; grandmother had told her grandson about how their leaves used to be harvested to feed silkworms. She actually took Luciano once to a village where they still farmed silk and he saw the trays of caterpillars spinning the cocoons that yield the fiber for textiles.

Other memories of his first times with grandmother surfaced in the boy's mind: the very first, sharp enough one was when, aged about three, he had been rushed back home from the river, soaked like a chick in the rain. While she undressed her amused little grandson in front of the fireplace, Giuseppina yelled at Luciano's Dad and his friend Camillo Vescovi because while they'd been mooring the boat they'd let him fall overboard - and it was winter!

That afternoon Luciano kept musing about his childhood. There was Ancona, the then frightening Wicked Queen in the movie "*Snow White and the Seven Dwarfs*"; the wrecked cars he loved so much, in the Palombina villa's garden; Venice - the trip there just before Dad left for Russia. Those recollections returned tantalizingly; he felt nostalgic about several enjoyable bygone moments, so different from the various current hardships. It was as if he could escape them by fleeing back in time - almost in search of refuge in serene recollections. The boy's memory, fumbling onwards for early pleasant moments, didn't omit his last boat trip with Dad in the fall of the previous year; that time they had gone upstream to the confluence. Once they got close enough, Mario moored the boat to a huge willow – further on the rapids were too strong - and helped his son climb up the steep left riverbank to a point where they had a good view of the two rivers merging. The water was quite high after rainfall the week before: the smaller River Bormida, which flowed fairly limpid and bluish-green over its gravelly bed, was squeezed against the right bank by the overwhelming, muddy Tanaro and shrank to nothing in a few hundred yards downstream. Luciano's continued meandering in his past, as if looking for a safe place to hide from the present day's threats, eventually evoked life in Belluno: the enchantment of the reveries suddenly burst and he was harshly brought back to his gloomy present.

Belluno: after stopping him just out of school that day at noon, they had questioned Luciano about Belluno too: was his father the *Federale* there (the top Fascist authority in town)? The boy had already met them some time the previous year: teenagers, only a little older than him and his close school friends, yet so different. They had not seemed threatening at the earlier encounters. They just seemed curious and Luciano didn't mind; on the contrary he felt proud and privileged to have lived in different regions of his home country and even more of his Dad - he liked to talk about that. However, just seeing those youths approaching him again that day, he felt uneasy, and there was soon plenty to worry about! Shortly the boy realized he was being held for unfriendly questioning about his Dad: he felt goose pimples. "When did you see him last time?".

"One week ago".

"Where is he now?"

"I don't know".

"Where has your father gone?" shouted another.

Luciano didn't answer and felt like crying, but bit his tongue.

"Show us what you've got in there!". He opened the cloth bag his parents had made, with the handle and frame recovered from a worn-out leather one: there were some comic books amongst the school items and they spotted one.

"We must seize those! That'll make you remember where your father has gone; you'd better!"

The school was housed in the same old municipal building in whose courtyard Luciano made his unlucky encounter with the youths who were questioning him. As people from the offices came out for their lunch break, the group holding the boy thought they'd better break up and let him go; his harassment most probably didn't last more than five minutes but he had felt it was endless. He might have reported that disturbing happening to his Mom, but she was away; he didn't mention it to grandmother or to aunt Tina when she returned from the hospital. Thus poor Luciano, already experiencing other hardships, got something more to worry about - running into those rascals again! He knew they would show up sooner or later and not long after that, in fact, they did.

When those young thugs who had kept Luciano on tenterhooks came back to see him after school, at first they pretended to approach him in a friendly way, but that was just while they made sure the municipal employees had all gone back inside to work. The boy, by no means reassured, noticed with more anxiety that Pistrullo had joined them. Pistrullo, nicknamed (like almost everyone in Pietra) because of his grandfather's surname Pistoja, was the ugliest human being Luciano could think of. Besides looking odd with his small baldish head, hooked nose and big jug ears, the same age as Luciano and like him skinny boy behaved badly. He lived close to Giuseppina's estate in a sinister-looking hut belonging to his grandfather, the village undertaker, partly hidden by small, bushy trees growing wild along the steep stairs leading up to the main square where the church and the town hall stood. Each time Luciano passed that hut, Pistrullo, playing truant, would stutter curses at him. Once he insulted Luciano's little sister who luckily enough couldn't understand any of the dirty words the rascal had uttered.

As some of the band of youths resumed questioning him, Luciano heard others briefing Pistrullo: "You know that f**king idiot is a Fascist? ... Don't you think we should teach him a lesson?" Pistrullo didn't answer but just sneered; then turned to Luciano and stuttered: "Blooo....blooody fassistsss!". Two of the youths held Luciano facing Pistrullo, each by an arm: "Come on! Don't be afraid - he can't hurt you!". Pistrullo moved close to the hapless hostage, muttered some gibberish and spat in his ashen face. Luciano felt a lump in his throat and his heart beating, strongly as never before, against his chest: the boys let him go. He wiped his face with his shirt sleeve. Pistrullo moved in even closer, facing him: Luciano, as if petrified, didn't back away. The two boys stood motionless really close, almost chest to chest, each with his arms hanging by his sides. The mobs incited Pistrullo once more: "Show him who you are!" Pistrullo bent his head slightly backward as if in scorn and challenge but then next, with a swift move, he bumped his forehead against Luciano's face. The crowd hailed their emboldened *protégé* who moved fast a few feet backward, raised his arms, waving them back and forth while bundling his hands into fists; that looked awkward and funny and somebody laughed, amid more hailing. Luciano tasted blood in his mouth and his tongue probed a cut in his upper lip.

Never before had he even witnessed a fight, let alone being caught in one. He had been taught to be gentle and that hurting anybody was reprehensible: an unforgivable sin. In his combat games, he never perceived war's true, innate evil of struggle, violence and murder; no-one suffered real injury and killing - it was all just for fun. Yet that blow from Pistrullo was real and wicked: the whole business with those youths was wicked and unfair. However, while he reflected on all this, Luciano – until then despairing - suddenly felt different. That hard blow which could have knocked him down, instead switched on an instinctive reaction compounding self-preservation, revolt, and anger: it turned him from fearful to furious. Finding it hard to believe himself, the boy all of a sudden ran at Pistrullo and jabbed his hand into his face, delivering quite a punch since Luciano's run had put a lot of extra strength into it! Pistrullo, whose nose was now bleeding badly, first faltered, then sat on the ground whinging; several from the crowd rushed to his rescue and the others followed. Momentarily nobody seemed to care about Luciano any longer: he grabbed his bag and fled home.

When grandmother saw her grandson arriving breathlessly, she set out to calm him but he couldn't speak; to her growing concern the boy began sobbing and wouldn't stop. There seemed to be no way Giuseppina could find out what had happened and even later, when aunt Tina came back from work, Luciano was still too upset. With much anguish though, in response to Tina's patient, reassuring insistence he began his "confession" and the more he told her about the trouble, the better he felt. Before that unforeseen scuffle with Pistrullo and its even less expected outcome, Luciano had just worried about himself. Now his main concern became how badly he had hurt his "contender" and guilty feelings prevailed. Aunt Tina comforted him best, first by saying it was a case of unintentional harm in self-defence; she added that a nosebleed after a blow doesn't usually last long and is of no concern: a little bother that soon rights itself, as long as one doesn't keep blowing the nose. Tina also explained that the bleeding seemed impressive because the nose contains a lot of tiny blood vessels whose task is to warm up the air we inhale. This last hint of his aunt's on respiratory physiology aroused Luciano's curiosity and helped take his mind off his obsessive thoughts about that day's troubles. As a matter of fact it gave him the idea of learning more about how our body-machine works. He could ask Carlo, the doctor next door, and borrow the volume of the Boys' Encyclopedia dealing with life sciences again. Meanwhile grandmother went straight over to see her undertaker neighbor Mr. Pistoja, to make sure his grandson was all right; aunt Tina disagreed. In the next few days Giuseppina found out who were the boys in the mob and made sure with their families, on pain of taking legal action, that they would have never besiege her grandchild again.

When Luciano went next door to see Carlo and borrow one of the Boys' Encyclopedia volumes, the doctor was not yet back from the hospital; his wife, Renata, who knew that the boy missed both his parents, was especially cheery. The young lady asked whether he would like to join her on a trip to town where she was due shortly to make arrangements for resettling the coming fall. A few days later, Luciano eagerly got ready with his bike and rode to Alessandria with the charming young lady. The town looked quite different from his only previous visit with Dad: it was unbelievably lively and busy! He soon noted a puzzling sign painted on the walls of every block: TYPHUS AREA; this display of English was meaningless to him and neither Renata, nor anybody else later on, could help. Yet he knew enough about the deadly plague which was endemic there at the time. He never forgot it had taken away beautiful Giuseppina Procchio, the Pietra shop-owners' teenage daughter. The Allies were concerned about that health hazard, after they had had to deal with the 1944 typhus epidemic in Naples. Many years later, grown-up Luciano, while searching the world literature in the medical school library, came across the word "typhus" which brought back to his mind the meaning of the arcane signs he had struggled in vain to understand as a little boy!

Although there were only a few cars around town, the street were so crowded with people that Renata and Luciano decided to push their bikes rather than riding them any further. However, before proceeding on foot, Luciano had a lucky break in the heavy traffic he had never experienced before. He had just overtaken someone pushing a cart when he spotted an iconic WWII car, the U.S. Army green Willys jeep with a white star surrounded by a circle painted on its hood: that was specifically designed as an aerial recognition symbol. Stupefied by the sight, the boy stopped suddenly in admiration, still astride his bike, forgetting about the cart he had just overtaken, now following close behind, but luckily enough it managed not to hit him. The man pushing it yelled at the clumsy biker, but Renata's bright smile soon did a lot to calm the angry fellow. Luciano recognized the town's largest square, named after Giuseppe Garibaldi, the general and patriot who led the war which united Italy in a single kingdom in 1861. There, on his earlier trip with Dad, he had seen people practicing *tamburello*. Renata, a former art student, intended to introduce him to the remarkable architecture of the site, encircled by three imposing buildings erected in the last decades of the nineteenth century. Two of them, identical, face each other along the opposite sides - around 200 yards long - of the rectangular square. A shorter building (half as long) stands at a right angle to the long ones and is very like them except for a huge clock towering high up in the center. The ground floors, mostly housing shops and the *mezzanine* floors above, are shaded by an arcade topped by two main storeys each with several balconies. The buildings had survived the war virtually unscarred. However, that day the square hosted a market which was busy and noisy, like something Luciano had never seen or heard before; besides vegetables and other foodstuffs, all sort of items were sold there. No wonder that aroused his curiosity so much that Renata's efforts to teach him about one of the city's landmarks were completely thwarted! However, she was so kind and let the boy take a long stroll into the midst of what to her seemed a completely unenticing hurly-burly.

It was probably there that Luciano first saw the AM-lire, the military currency interchangeable with the normal Italian lira, put into circulation by the Allies in Italy after their landing in Sicily in July 1943.

They contributed to the high inflation that hit Italy towards the end of World War II, even more so since the AM-lire were falsified on a large scale! The occupiers' currency looked quite different from the somber Italian banknotes he was familiar with, the dark bluish ten-lire bill depicting the king's head and shoulders on one side, within two Fascist symbols. The smaller denomination AM-lire bills, 1, 2, 5 and 10, were square and had only the value written in numbers and in Italian in black on a bright multicolored background. On the back you could read in English the Four Freedoms (of speech and religion, and from want, and fear) enshrined in the United States Constitution. Some U.S. Army surplus was already being sold at that market, including chewing gum Luciano had never heard of it. Renata bought him some and later on aunt Tina disapproved! Next to the chewing gum Luciano spotted some condoms in a basket marked *preservativi americani* and asked Renata about them, but she didn't reply. He didn't miss, though, the fact that his "chaperon" and the vendor there exchanged a sort of knowing smile; the latter also muttered something like: "Nowadays these boys are impatient to grow up!". Luciano played along and begged Renata to let him have a look at the place where he was to stay when school began in September that year. Meanwhile he made a mental note of her previous reticence: that was most probably the kind of prickly adult matter he had better approach with cousin Gabriele's help!

Grandpa Joe's apartment building was where Luciano's family intended to move in September; the site had been heavily bombed. One side of the three-storey building stood at a corner where two streets crossed and was badly scarred because the house it faced had been destroyed by a bomb; most balconies had lost their railings, and fixtures were missing or falling apart. The best-preserved side was the opposite one facing the courtyard, looking onto the other street, with a kind of arcade comprising the gate and topped by an ample terrace which was part of the first floor apartment where Luciano's family was intending to settle. Renata noted the boy didn't really look very keen on the place (he had just been impressed by what was shortly to be the lady's fancy residence in *Corso Roma*, Alessandria's main street): "Your mother will make a beautiful garden on that terrace!" she said to cheer him up. Eventually Renata proved right, but for at least a year the terrace hosted only the poultry Luciano's mom took along from Pietra: a real blessing as long as hand-to-mouth times lasted!

That trip to town with the kindly young lady was good for Luciano. After his recent, depressing setbacks it offered the boy a sort of silver lining, the prospect of a fresh life in Alessandria, with plenty to discover, and meeting new friends. But the recovery from wartime hardship in the town took some time and at first meant further "endurance" for Luciano and his family who didn't escape poverty right away. Dad started teaching maths in a priests' college in Tortona where he had been taught about three decades before, but that hardly made ends meet. The unwary boy sadly experienced shameful mocking in front of the class by his 5th grade school teacher, Mr. Demichelis; he eventually told his parents, but they could only regret being compelled to act as if nothing had happened and explained that it was because the nasty individual knew Dad had been a Fascist.

In September 1946 Luciano easily passed the exam for admission to high school and early the following year his father exploited his own university degree and long managerial experience by getting a high-earning job; meanwhile mother had started gardening on the terrace and the family enjoyed an ice box. Like most of those who had survived the war in good health, the Manara family's life got better each day against the backdrop of what was then dubbed the Italian "economic miracle". Substantial help came with the Marshall Plan, the U.S. support scheme to rebuild the post-war European economies in order to prevent the spread of Soviet Communism.

Long afterwards Luciano happened to recall gratefully the comforting bike trip to Alessandria in the aftermath of World War II to the by then white-haired Renata, when already sporting a salt-and-pepper look himself!

17. Animal Farm

The boys got there in mid morning after less than ten minutes' uphill walk from the farm; it was a partly shrubby area several times larger than the farm's ample barnyard and, like it, carved into a hillside. All around gentle slopes ran down, circling the site, except on its west side where the rest of the hill rose sharply like a wall. You could see the top of a man-made hole, just above the ground, overlooking the bushes. That was the opening of a long-abandoned limestone pit; the old cement plant, in fact, could be spotted far away down in the plains alongside the road to town. It didn't matter whether those boys had been severely warned against playing around there, by whoever was concerned with each of them, and in the most convincing way. On that mid-morning of an early September day, all three of them had gathered at "*la cava*" (literally, the quarry), as the pit was known, for a precise reason: the expedition was meant to take place then, once and for ever! Luciano knew that in a few days he would have to leave to go back to school far away.

The "explorers" rested a short while in front of the pit opening where, amid some rubble, there were the remains of who knows what appliance involved in the works once carried on there. The sun, still far from its zenith, lit up the first few feet of the tunnel into the pit, whose view, if not exactly enticing, didn't scare those intending to enter too much either. Luciano, the leader, delivering his briefing, first cheered Pasqualino for carrying the rolled rope he had ordered him to provide, by taking down the long washing line the women used to stretch across a corner of the barnyard for hanging laundry to dry. Then he showed how he would wear one of the rope's ends around his waist as if it were a belt, and fastened it. In turn Pasqualino was supposed to do the same, after releasing some ten more yards of rope. The remaining rolled rope was to be carried by the third boy, Mio. Only the first two boys were supposed to walk into the pit side by side, while carefully holding the portion of the rope linking them, so as

139

to prevent it getting tangled in any encumbrances possibly left on the floor of the tunnel. Mio's watch role consisted in releasing the rope as the two entrants pulled it so as to keep it stretched enough. Signalling through the rope was: one tug, release the rope; two tugs, recover it. Years later Luciano in high school had some nostalgic feelings of *déjà vu* because of those games at *la cava:* they were translating from Latin Ovid's Metamorphoses about Adriadne's myth whereby Theseus, once he had killed the Minotaur, found his way back out again by following her thread which he had let unwind through the labyrinth.

That day's gang was well assorted. Luciano, after the dismay of the last events of the war and its immediate aftermath, had re-acquired self-confidence with his peers and enjoyed the new pals; his revived fantasy and imagination fed most of the new games he involved them in. Pasqualino was a sort of naive enthusiast who would back any of Luciano's suggestions, no matter how hazardous; finally Mio was the wise one in the party. Unlike the temporary guests at the farm, Luciano and Pasqualino - the latter was hosted by his aunt living in a hut some hundred yards from the farm's barnyard - Mio belonged to a family working there for the farm's owners; often he didn't join the other boys in their leisure because he had to help his parents and relatives in the fields and vineyards. With that experience, although he was the same age as the other two, he was more grown-up and most of the time prudent enough to discourage them from doing anything potentially troublesome. Mio had voted against exploring the *cava* but he arranged nonetheless to be there on "D day", to keep an eye on his less cautious little friends.

No ill fate loomed yet in the tube - just disappointment. The two "pioneers" heartbreakingly moved a few steps slowly into the tube; they stumbled awkwardly over rubble, but felt confident enough to carry on. The light started to get dim as they advanced and shortly it was hard to see what they were stepping on. At that point Luciano, who was less than one step ahead, stopped Pasqualino on his side, by raising his arm across his friend's chest; he looked back for a while at the lighted opening, an impressive view which, however, further reduced his ability to see in the dark. Then he remembered a trick his dad had taught him when they descended together into grandfather Joe's majestic cave: keep your eyes tight closed for a couple of minutes. Both the boys did so and could see a little farther, just in time not to bump into a wall-like bulk of rubble which blocked the way; it was time for an uneventful but honourable retreat!

When they checked how much rope Mio had rolled out, it came out as a mere 60 feet. It was Mio who made the only discovery of the day: on removing some rubble at the entrance, an iron bar emerged in the ground, running on into the tube, most probably one of a pair forming the track for the carts which carried the pit's ores.

Having deemed their mission accomplished, the boys turned merrily back to the farm. As directed by Mio, they made a stop at a vineyard and helped themselves to some delicious white grapes. When they got in sight of the farm, near enough to be seen themselves, they spotted Cini, the not yet five-year-old "boss" there, wielding a whip: that was the kind of welcome to avoid, at least for Pasqualino and Mio!

Luciano had been brought there in August 1945, just when, after some difficulty finding a publisher, George Orwell's masterpiece "Animal Farm" appeared. The book, somehow like the works of the legendary ancient authors Phaedrus and Aesop, centers on fictional beasts to portray human vices; it censures the Bolshevik Revolution and its subversion into Stalin's oppressive dictatorship, in the guise of a fable about a group of barnyard animals. The animals Luciano became familiar with at "Bricco San Michele" (bricco means hill), a real farm, were natural and by no means intent to overthrow their owners; but let us begin with the site and the humans.

The Davico family's property was in the foothills of the Ligurian Apennines, southeast of Pietra Marazzi, Luciano's ancestors' village, wherefrom they can be seen in a crystal-clear day. The mountain range, starting from about Savona, runs eastbound bordering the Mediterranean Sea to the Gulf of Genoa, separating it from the upper Po Valley; it follows the line of the Bormida River; then bends away to southeast and continues along the whole length of peninsular Italy like its backbone. The Bricco consisted of a whole hill, mainly cultivated as vineyards, and of more cultivable land in the lower-stretching valley, where runs a creek, the Grue. It looked as if most of the upper part of the hill had been carved as a flat surface to accommodate the buildings and the barnyard; a bit like at the "cava", its northern edge was the wall-like slope to the top of the hill. The buildings, including in a single body housing for the owners and farmers, stables and stores with haylofts above them, sided the slope (possibly a shield from the north winds). On the opposite side, there was another imposing three-story building sitting unfinished; it was to be opened years later with an unforgettable party.

The housing section reserved for the owners and their guests was welcoming and comfortable, but no tap water or electricity was available at the time; fine old furniture, paintings and petrol lamps at night evoked the atmosphere of a movie of the past and Signora Matilde Lugano, the oldest dweller, in her late sixties, dressed the same way all the time. The white-haired lady, a widow, was of gentle birth and her manners inspired respect and authority; at the same time she always presented an encouraging, sincere smile, even when discreetly manifesting her discontent. It didn't look as though Matilde was concerned with running the farm; however there was no doubt that she had the final say on any major issue in her household.

It must have been like this when the Davicos offered hospitality to Luciano's Dad Mario, hiding from the post-war bloody revenges against the Fascists. In a few weeks of turmoil from late April 1945, following the end of the second world conflict in northern Italy, the toll of slaughter might have been as high as 10,000. For decades that shameful page of 20th century history remained untold. It was only in the years 2000 that Giampaolo Pansa, a renowned Italian journalist, published several most successful books on the subject, based on eye witness accounts and letters of those times. Hosting one of the potential victims of those revenges could have cost the Davicos the burning of their property if not their own life; Luciano gratefully never forgot that!

Signora Matilde had three sons and a daughter, Carla, probably the last-born, who lived with her new family in a vast farm near Sale, a village midway between Bricco San Michele and Pietra Marazzi, where Luciano's Dad first hid. Matilde's oldest son Luigi, known as Gino, was a tall, handsome, sturdy auburn-haired man; around 45 at the time, he ran the farm, much respected by those working there because he used to go first whenever risky jobs required it and always knew what to do, either if a cow was in trouble giving birth to her calf, or any machinery had broken down. Gino, an ardent hunter, had many professional friends, like doctors and lawyers who occasionally came to the farm; he never meddled in politics or married, although it seem he was quite successful with women, generally those much younger than him: he became Luciano's idol.

Matilde's second-born, black-haired Vittorio, was a teacher who was not involved in the farm; he had just come back from Sardinia after being a prisoner of war of U.S. troops, as a captain in the Italian Royal Army. It was because of his acquaintance with Vittorio, who as a teacher must have been linked to the Opera Balilla, that Luciano's father, Mario, was offered the Davicos' life-saving hospitality. The youngest of the three brothers never came back from the Russian front; his daughter, little Matilde, known as Cini, was born after he left.

The girl's mother, Mariuccia, was a charming young woman under thirty; other women at the farm helped her with the housekeeping, but nonetheless she was busy all day long: she baked bread and pies and fixed tasty meals.

Everybody liked Luciano, including Cini who admired him; but she was quite a character and more than once dealing with her obliged him to keep his temper. The enchanting beauty of the tiny ash-blond, angel-faced, blue-eyed creature only just concealed a strong personality surprisingly developed for an under-five girl. Cini, who sported small braids, either combed over her head or as pigtails, most of the time stayed with the adults (who adored her); constantly exposed to their talk, the girl at times sounded as if she were an adult herself. In essence she tended to do only what she liked: there was no way out of that without upsetting her - not a rare occurrence.

Luciano had no recollections of dolls and the like belonging to his little landlady companion - possibly she fancied toy guns! Other girls at the farm were grown up enough to help their families rather than play with Cini, who was always looking for Mio and Pasqualino, then Luciano, and drove all of them at her discretion. With the first two, occasionally she was surprisingly rude considering her near-angelic appearance. In any case the interests she liked the boys to join in with were rather male-oriented; one day in the fields Luciano was a bit shocked to see her pee standing like a boy - but that was just the first time. As an adult Cini proved a typical Italian woman of her times; she married young, had four children including twins, and spent most of her time caring for her new family and the aging one where she grew up.

The Davicos talked to each other in the local dialect (from Tortona), but never to Cini and at dinner as long as she was there. The little girl used to get up at dawn and didn't take a daytime nap, so she would fall asleep shortly after dinner was served. None of the Davicos ever spoke to Luciano in dialect, but his father, who was raised in Tortona till a teenager, eagerly joined his hosts' usual conversation all day long. Luciano had acquired a fair understanding of the dialect in Pietra (which, however, he could hardly speak) and pretended to go along with the local one. One day, however, Gino tested him: there was a funnel left on the table and he asked the boy (in Italian): "Would you please pass me the *pidariò*?". Dad smiled and Luciano looked around haplessly: a funnel in Pietra was called *turtrò*! In Piedmont, like in many other Italian regions, the dialects of dwellers in places no more than a few miles apart may differ a lot. After World War Two, however, partly because of substantial migration within the country, dialects were spoken less and less up, even facing extinction in many places towards the end of the century. Yet they have some chance of surviving for a while as world-renowned authors of the past, like the Venetian comedian Carlo Goldoni, have written some of their works in dialect.

The animals were no doubt Luciano's major attraction at the Bricco; most he knew already, but he had plenty of opportunities for closer encounters (even too close!). The number of poultry wandering freely all around in the fields and vineyards in daytime was impressive; one could hardly walk through when, in the evening, they gathered in the barnyard to shelter in their huts from the foxes. Luciano had never seen guinea hens before; they resembled game birds and as fast flyers used to roam far away from the farm. Luciano had never seen a mule either, the offspring of a male donkey and a female horse; at the farm there was Pirro, always confined in his pen - most probably he wasn't tame enough. His mother, Nella, looked like a quiet animal, but animals are still animals and one never knows them well enough
to foresee the threats they may pose! Bovines abounded: cows bred calves and provided milk; oxen, the only source of traction power beside Nella, worked hard most of the year pulling ploughs, threshers and carts. Tilling was almost all on steep slopes, ideal for sunny vineyards but managing heavily loaded carts, like at vintage time, was no joke.
Of course in a place almost in the middle of nowhere like the Bricco, wildlife spread at will and, believe it or not, Cini knew a lot about them - mostly game birds, as taught by uncle Gino; thanks to her, Luciano learned how to recognize birds at a distance by the way they fly. She also occasionally pointed out the ground openings of shelters dug out by badgers or foxes as well as their trails through the wilderness.

A major development with the farm animals was when Luciano, who had long begged to be allowed, was given permission to drive the cattle out to graze. There was really nothing extraordinary about this. Once the animals were let out of the barn, they knew what to do: go along the north side of the barnyard till the corner with the east and take the steeply descending northbound trail to the "Scavino" (a small carving - every place at the farm had a name), a westward extending terrace about the size of the barnyard, no more than two hundred yards away. There was mostly clover, a delicacy for the cattle, but a few rows of vines stretched along the terrace's northern edge. While the animals Luciano had followed enjoyed their meal, he would lie back, feeling pleased with himself, in the shade of a tree and let his fantasy roam at leisure. In the late afternoon, when daylight started to dim, the herd would spontaneously turn back home, proudly followed by its attendant. He liked his quasi-cowboy appointment, but something was missing: a horse. So he started to beg for that too; he didn't want to ride one - all he wanted was that Nella could join the grazing cattle. It didn't take too long for Luciano to persuade the farmers there was nothing wrong with letting that big quiet mare come along with the cattle - but that was a mistake! The horse's company, meant to make the boy's bucolic experience more enjoyable, came close to turning into a tragedy, all because of those few rows of vines stretched along one edge of the clover field. Luciano knew some of the best table grapes were picked there. That afternoon the boy lay once more on the grass with the herd grazing; up in the clear blue September sky, white clouds gently sailing by unfolding in different shapes; their view suggested several enchanting resemblances to him. Glancing towards the animals, however, all of a sudden the boy was shaken out of his idyllic fantasies: Nella had wandered over to the vines and was feeding on them. It was a matter of seconds: he, who had never been warned: "Never go close to the hind legs of a horse!", was there wielding the stick he took along when on those herding trips and hit the animal's buttocks with all his might. It must have been like an explosion as the horse kicked, lashing out with her sledge-hammer-like hooves. Luciano was found lying several feet away only at sunset, after the herd had gone back to the farm without him.

Several factors (the light weight of the skinny boy offering minimal resistance to the blow, which mostly turned into kinetic energy; his distance from the kicking horse; the non-vital site of impact on his body, a thigh, hit sidewise by only one hoof) probably accounted for his miraculously mild injuries. This considering the destructive potential of an equine back kick which, they say, compares to the impact of an automobile moving at 30 kilometers per hour! When Luciano, in bed, silent, confused and suffering, showed signs of being fairly aware of his whereabouts once more, dad and Gino were bent over him: it was a difficult moment for both of them. They could only dream of getting a doctor there, and wondered whether and how to take the boy to a hospital. Dad was holding Luciano's cold hands; Gino cautiously checked the boy's condition in search of some reassuring signs. There were no visible signs of the sites of impact except for a bit bruise on the upper right thigh; he also slid gently both hands over the boy's abdomen, which did not seem tight or painful. Luciano was given a spoonful of milk, which he swallowed; when Gino eventually left, he nodded first to indicate his confidence in a favourable outcome to Mario who kept his son's hands in his own until the boy fell asleep. In about a week Luciano could walk almost like before and shortly later run even faster; however, it took him some time to look at the large animals there like he used to before, not just Nella, but for a long time later on just the view of other horses unsettled him. Yet he was told that what Nella did was an unconscious reaction: the animal never had the intention of hitting him.

Luciano's feeling for Nella had been "love at first sight". Shortly after his arrival at the Bricco, in the last week of August, the nearby city of Tortona was celebrating its main religious feast honouring Our Lady of Guardia and the Davicos were expected there. Gino had set up their imposing coach which much impressed Luciano and his excitement grew when the man brought in Nella to equip her. The boy had never seen such a large, handsome equine so close, her big, glossy eyes inspiring confidence. Gino was carefully fitting her with all those forms of horse tack, like headgear, reins and harness, while curious Luciano asked and eagerly learned what they were for. Nella patiently waited to be ready; she almost looked proud tacked up wit all those fine implements. When everybody got on the open coach, it moved slowly across the barnyard to the southbound driveway which, at Pasqualino's aunt's hut, made an almost U-turn to continue down on a frighteningly steep, long, straight tract going almost all the way to the valley bottom; there it joined the main road to Tortona. From the driver's seat whose handles Luciano clung to, next to Gino, the trail looked even steeper. The carriage, however, advanced unfaltering as the skilled Gino gauged the brake and Nella wisely let the crowded coach move downhill at the appropriate pace: a safe ride thanks to an accomplished man-animal interaction. Along the main road in the plain Gino handed the reins to Luciano, telling him to keep them loose, since the horse knew the way; the boy nonetheless felt great, as if assigned a responsible task and turned his head back towards the passengers, looking for his Dad's nod.

The time finally came for Luciano to leave the Bricco and go back to school in Alessandria in mid-September. After the few weeks of turmoil at the end of April, the rule of law resumed gradually; armed bands no longer lorded it, having dissolved with the arrival of the Allies, who left soon thereafter, once regular police forces were restored; the "People's Tribunal" had been suppressed. On the day of farewell Luciano and his Dad recovered their bicycles and packed only a few clean clothes; Signora Matilde kindly gave them a small sack full of nuts. There was no reason for a heart-rending goodbye, because it was clear that the hosts and their guests would meet again and again lifelong: some tears fell though. Since the downhill trail could not be seen from the barnyard, Cini and her mother strolled, with father and son, as far as the turn in the driveway at the hut; they looked at those departing, walking away slowly without daring to ride their bikes down that frighteningly steep path. Mario and Luciano went down following their increasingly long mid-afternoon shadows till Cini could barely spot them and they faded in her shining eyes.

Index

Printed in the United States
By Bookmasters